Walter Rauschenbusch

WALTER RAUSCHENBUSCH

Essential Spiritual Writings

Selected with an Introduction by

JOSEPH J. FAHEY

ORBIS BOOKS
Maryknoll, New York 10545

ORBIS BOOKS
Maryknoll, New York 10545

Founded in 1970, Orbis Books endeavors to publish works that enlighten the mind, nourish the spirit, and challenge the conscience. The publishing arm of the Maryknoll Fathers and Brothers, Orbis seeks to explore the global dimensions of the Christian faith and mission, to invite dialogue with diverse cultures and religious traditions, and to serve the cause of reconciliation and peace. The books published reflect the views of their authors and do not represent the official position of the Maryknoll Society. To learn more about Maryknoll and Orbis Books, please visit our website at www.maryknollsociety.org.

Library of Congress Cataloging-in-Publication Data

Names: Rauschenbusch, Walter, 1861–1918, author. | Fahey, Joseph, editor.
Title: Walter Rauschenbusch : essential spiritual writings / selected with an introduction by Joseph J. Fahey.
Description: Maryknoll : Orbis Books, 2019. | Series: Modern spiritual masters series | Includes bibliographical references.
Identifiers: LCCN 2019017879 (print) | LCCN 2019020363 (ebook) | ISBN 9781608338108 (ebook) | ISBN 9781626983465 (print)
Subjects: LCSH: Social gospel. | Theology.
Classification: LCC BT738 (ebook) | LCC BT738 .R343 2019 (print) | DDC 230/.61--dc23
LC record available at https://lccn.loc.gov/2019017879

Contents

To my Maryknoll Seminary Professors

Norbert Fleckenstein, M.M.
William Frazier, M.M.
William McCarthy, M.M.
John McConnell, M.M.
George Putnam, M.M.

In gratitude to these fine priests
and to all Maryknollers
who taught me to seek first
the Reign of God.

Preface

In 1958 I entered the seminary to study for the priesthood with the Maryknoll Fathers, a Roman Catholic missionary order. Prior to that I attended twelve years of Catholic education at Holy Family School and St. Helena's High School, both in the Bronx, New York. When I left Maryknoll a year before ordination in 1966 to teach Theology at Manhattan College, I had a solid grounding in traditional Catholic education. I memorized the Baltimore Catechism in grade school, and in high school I took courses that included apologetics—the science of explaining and defending the Catholic faith. Yet I knew next to nothing about Protestantism except that heretics were going to hell and Catholic apostates (those who had *fallen* from the faith) would join them. Jews were rarely discussed, and I recall feeling sorry for them because they rejected Christ who was one of their own. My only knowledge of Muslims was that they fought our glorious Catholic Crusaders in the medieval period. Overall, my twelve years of Catholic education were hardly friendly to those who did not belong to my church, which I was taught was the Kingdom of God on earth and the only vehicle to salvation.

In the seminary I took traditional courses in philosophy such as cosmology, metaphysics, epistemology, theodicy, and logic. In theological studies I was taught Old and New Testaments, patristics (the fathers of the early church), church history, dogmatic theology, missiology, moral theology, and canon law, among other topics. While we received a solid grounding in scripture and theology, we only superficially studied Protestant theology and, while we were honestly taught that a reformation was necessary in the church, we did not go into any depth in the study of the Reformation theologians or churches.

Through my years in Maryknoll we also took courses in economics, sociology, politics, and psychology, which did not then exist in many traditional Catholic seminaries. (In fact, in 1960 I remember telling my pastor at home in the Bronx that I was taking sociology and psychology, and he was horrified. "Sociology will turn you into a Marxist and psychology will teach you that sin doesn't exist!" he thundered.) Even the study of scripture, examining the historical and cultural context of events in the Bible, was frowned upon by some traditionalists in the 1960s.

My theological studies coincided exactly with the years of the Second Vatican Council (1962–1965). We studied *leaked* Vatican statements on everything from the church in the modern world to liturgical practice. Many of us enthusiastically welcomed the changes in the church by good Pope John XXIII, who sought to open the windows of the church to the wonderful things that were going on in God's world, a world that was wider than the Catholic Church. We were taught the then-novel insight that in fact the Reign of God was wider than the church and that, as missionaries, we were not only bringing God's Kingdom to "pagan" lands, but also discovering the Reign of God already at work there.

When I decided to pursue a PhD, I chose to enter the program in Religion at New York University that included my chosen field of Christian Social Ethics, along with studies in world religions and, especially, courses in Protestant theological ethics at New York's Union Theological Seminary. Union was the home of such famous Protestant scholars as Paul Tillich, Reinhold Niebuhr, and John C. Bennett, among many other luminaries. While taking a course with Professor Bennett on Christian Ethics and International Affairs I encountered for the first time the social ethics of Reinhold Niebuhr and also studied the German martyr Dietrich Bonhoeffer. In my studies on Niebuhr I encountered a name I had never heard before: Walter Rauschenbusch. I immediately was drawn to the Social Gospel and the conviction that the Reign of God was meant for this earth.

Although I wrote my dissertation on Niebuhr, I never forgot my fondness for the Social Gospel, which, unfortunately, Niebuhr came to criticize. I came to believe that Niebuhr did not fairly represent Rauschenbusch and the Social Gospel Movement. I believe it is time to recover Rauschenbusch's inspiring and, yes, realistic message for the crises that beset us in the twenty-first century.

It has been a delight, while compiling this book, to once again explore Rauschenbusch and his still relevant call to advance the Reign of God here on earth in our time and for the generations to come.

I am grateful to Robert Ellsberg, the publisher of Orbis Books, for his encouragement with this book and his wise and constructive editing of my work. Thanks also to all the fine people at Orbis who make works such as this possible and who contribute to Rauschenbusch's ideal of establishing the Reign of God here on earth. Thanks to my good friends, Paul Dinter, Joe Holland, and Kate Shanley for their thoughtful comments and constructive criticism of my writing and work. Thanks also to Professor Melanie A. Duguid-May of Colgate Rochester Crozer Divinity School for assistance in understanding Rauschenbusch's concept of Original Sin and Baptist teaching on this matter. Mistakes, of course, are my own.

Key Dates in the Life of Walter Rauschenbusch

1861   Walter Rauschenbusch was born on October 4, 1861, in Rochester, NY. His father, August Rauschenbusch came to the United States from Germany as a Lutheran pastor who later became a Baptist because he thought their spirituality and governance closer to the New Testament ideal.

1879–1883   After completing primary education in the United States, Rauschenbusch attends college in Germany at *Evangelishe Gymnasium zu Gutersloh* in Westphalia between Cologne and Berlin. He studies liberal arts with a strong focus on the classics, and is exposed to the emerging social sciences of political economy and sociology that were pioneered in German universities.

1883–1886   Rauschenbusch attends Rochester Theological Seminary in New York to pursue studies as a Baptist minister. He studies Old Testament, biblical literature and New Testament exegesis, ecclesiastical history, mental and moral philosophy, and Greek, Latin, and German, among many traditional seminary courses.

1886–1897   Pastor at the Second Baptist Church in the Hell's Kitchen section of New York City. Rauschenbusch experiences firsthand the misery of workers, victims of predatory capitalists, who exploit the poor in the pursuit of ever greater wealth. He is pastor to people who work ten- to twelve-hour six-day workweeks and who live in unsafe and unsanitary tenements. He is particularly moved by the funerals of young children who are the special victims of capitalist neglect. He calls himself a Christian Socialist and urges worker ownership of the means of production.

1887   Rauschenbusch is strongly influenced by the thought of Henry George and Catholic priest Father Edward McGlynn on the *single tax*. He is a founder of a Baptist reflection group that he calls the Society of Jesus. It is inspired by Jesuit spirituality.

1891   Rauschenbusch takes a sabbatical in Germany where he formulates his doctrine on the Kingdom of God on earth as central to the Christian mission. He writes *Christianity Revolutionary* which is not published in his lifetime. He also visits England to study the Salvation Army, British socialism, and the worker cooperatives of Robert Owen and the Rochdale Pioneers.

1892   Rauschenbusch is a founder of the Brotherhood of the Kingdom along with other Baptist pastors to propagate the Reign of God on earth as the hallmark of the Social Gospel.

1893   Rauschenbusch marries Pauline Rother. They have five children: Winifred, Hilmar, Paul, Karl, and Elizabeth.

1897–1918   Rauschenbusch spends his remaining years as a professor at Rochester Theological Seminary where he teaches courses in church history and Christian ethics. He is a strong advocate of a historical and cultural understanding of the New Testament and supports the emerging social sciences of political economy, sociology, and psychology.

1907   Publication of Rauschenbusch's most famous work, *Christianity and the Social Crisis*. 50,000 copies are very quickly in print. Rauschenbusch is on the lecture circuit almost weekly for several years after its publication.

1910   Publication of *Prayers of the Social Awakening*, perhaps his most spiritual work. The book is very popular in Protestant churches and on university campuses.

1912   Publication of *Christianizing the Social Order*. Rather that calling for a theocracy, Rauschenbusch offers practical insights on how the economy might be improved with Christian values. He holds, "A private business that employs thousands of people, uses the natural resources of the nation, enjoys exemptions and privileges at law, and is essential to the welfare of great communities is not a private business. It is public, and the sooner we abandon the fiction that it is private, the better for our common sense."

1914   Publication of *Dare We Be Christians?* This is one of Rauschenbusch's most spiritual works that focuses on love as the central force in building the Kingdom of God on earth. He states, "Our understanding of life depends on our comprehension of the universal powers of love. Our capacity to build society depends on our power of calling out love. Our faith in God and Christ is measured by our faith in the value and workableness of love."

1916   Publication of *The Social Principles of Jesus*. Written for college students, this practical text proves very popular, and 15,000 copies are printed in the first three months. The book consists of daily readings and case studies that focuses on forming students for a life of public service.

1917   Publication of *A Theology for the Social Gospel*. This last book is written, in part, to answer Rauschenbusch's critics that he and the Social Gospel do not deal sufficiently with the reality of sin in human affairs. He speaks of the solidarity of sin and refers to the Kingdom of Evil but rejects Original Sin as the biological transmission of sin.

1918   Dies on July 25, 1918.

Sources

A Theology for the Social Gospel (1917), https://archive.
org/stream/theologyfortheso002843mbp/theologyfortheso002843mbp_djvu.txt.

Christianity and the Social Crisis (1907), https://archive.org/
details/christianitysoci00rausiala/page/n6.

Christianity Revolutionary (1891), published posthumously as
The Righteousness of the Kingdom, ed. Max L. Stackhouse
(Nashville: Abingdon Press, 1968).

Christianizing the Social Order (1912), https://archive.org/
details/christianizingso00rausiala/page/n8.

Dare We Be Christians? (1914), https://archive.org/details/darewebechristia00rausuoft/page/n10.

For God and the People: Prayers of the Social Awakening
(1910), https://archive.org/details/forgodpeoplepray00raus/
page/n8.

Prayers of the Social Awakening (1910), https://archive.org/
details/prayersofsociala00rausiala/page/n8.

"The New Evangelism," *The Independent*, Vol. 56, Issues 2888-
2900, May 1904. https://tinyurl.com/yxzacvax.

The Social Principles of Jesus (1916), https://archive.org/details/
socialprinciples00raus/page/n6.

Works Cited

Brackney, William H., ed. 2018. *Walter Rauschenbusch: Published Works and Selected Writings in Three Volumes.* Macon, GA: Mercer University Press.

Crossan, John Dominic. 1994. *Jesus: A Revolutionary Biography.* Sonoma, CA: Polebridge Press.

Deichman Edwards, Wendy J., and Carolyn De Swarte Gifford. 2003. *Gender and the Social Gospel.* Urbana: University of Illinois Press.

Dorrien, Gary Dorrien. 2003. *The Making of American Liberal Theology: Idealism, Realism, and Modernity.* Louisville, KY: Westminster John Knox Press.

Evans, Christopher H. 2004. *The Kingdom Is Always but Coming: A Life of Walter Rauschenbusch.* Grand Rapids, MI: William B. Eerdmans.

———. 2017. *The Social Gospel in American Religion: A History.* New York: New York University Press.

George, Henry. 1879. *Progress and Poverty,* New York: E. P. Dutton & Co.

Gutiérrez, Gustavo. 1973. *A Theology of Liberation: History, Politics, and Salvation.* Maryknoll, NY: Orbis Books.

Hudson, Winthrop H. 1984. *Walter Rauschenbusch: Selected Writings.* New York: Paulist Press.

King Jr., Martin Luther. 1958. *Stride toward Freedom.* Publisher unknown.

Niebuhr, Reinhold. 1964. *The Nature and Destiny of Man.* New York: Charles Scribner's Sons.

Pope John XXIII. 1963. http://w2.vatican.va/content/john-xxiii/en/encyclicals/documents/hf_j-xxiii_enc_11041963_pacem.html.

Pope Paul VI. 1965. *Gaudium et Spes.* http://www.vatican.va/archive/hist_councils/ii_vatican_council/documents/vat-ii_const_19651207_gaudium-et-spes_en.html.

Ryan, John A., with an introduction by Richard T. Ely. 1906. *A Living Wage: Its Ethical and Economic Aspects.* New York: Macmillan.

United States Catholic Bishops. 1986. "Economic Justice for All: Pastoral Letter on Catholic Social Teaching and the U.S. Economy." http://www.usccb.org/upload/economic_justice_for_all.pdf.

Wink, Walter. 2003. *Jesus and Nonviolence: A Third Way.* Minneapolis: Fortress.

World Synod of Bishops. 1971. "Justice in the World." https://www1.villanova.edu/content/dam/villanova/mission/JusticeIntheWorld1971.pdf.

Introduction

Blessed are you poor, for yours is the kingdom of God.
Blessed are you that hunger now, for you shall be
satisfied.
Blessed are you that weep now, for you shall laugh.
                        —Jesus of Nazareth (Luke 6:20–21)

The Spirit of God is moving men in our generation
toward a better understanding of the idea of the Kingdom of God on earth. Obeying the thought of our Master, and trusting in the power and guidance of the Spirit,
we form ourselves into a Brotherhood of the Kingdom,
in order to reestablish this idea in the thought of the
church, and to assist in its practical realization in the life
of the world.   —Walter Rauschenbusch

Brotherhood of the Kingdom (1892 statement)

It has been my conviction ever since reading Rauschenbusch that any religion which professes to be concerned
about the soul of men and is not concerned about the
social and economic conditions that scar that soul, is a
spiritually moribund religion waiting for the day to be
buried.   —Martin Luther King Jr. *Stride toward Freedom* (1958)

Walter Rauschenbusch (1861–1918) and the Social Gospel that
he championed are well known in Protestant theological circles.
Most ministers in various denominations have studied the Social
Gospel in seminary, and some regularly preach the Social Gospel

in their churches. Even in its rejection by certain contemporary *prosperity gospel* preachers, homage is paid to a movement that dominated American Protestant thought in the late nineteenth and early twentieth centuries.

In contrast, Rauschenbusch and the Social Gospel are hardly known in Roman Catholic circles. There was a time when Catholic university students would have been familiar with the Catholic *social gospel* through study of such documents as Pope Leo XIII's 1891 encyclical *Rerum Novarum*—"On the Condition of the Working Classes"—and the writings of Father John A. Ryan in the first half of the twentieth century. That is much less likely today. And yet Rauschenbusch's message continues to bear a challenging and relevant message for today. It is my hope that this small collection of his writings will stir renewed interest by a generation of Christians who sorely need reminding of the revolutionary nature of Jesus's message and the mission of the Christian churches in seeking the Reign of God here on earth.

The foundational insight of the Social Gospel Movement was that Jesus's mission and message essentially concerned establishing the Kingdom of God here on earth. As Rauschenbusch noted, the "Our Father"—the only prayer that Jesus taught us—challenged us to build the Kingdom of God here "on earth as it is in heaven." Writing in *A Theology for the Social Gospel*, he argued that "the theological significance of the life of Christ has been comprised [*sic*] in the incarnation, the atonement, and the resurrection . . . The social gospel would interpret all the events of his life, including his death, by the dominant purpose which he consistently followed, the establishment of the Kingdom of God." This radical notion challenged the conservative Christian churches of the late nineteenth and early twentieth centuries with a stern critique of capitalism as well as a hearty defense of the exploited masses. According to Walter Rauschenbusch and the Social Gospelers, the Good News that Jesus proclaimed was intended to radically transform the economic, political, and social structures of life *here on earth*. The mission of the Christian church was to participate in the creation of the Kingdom of God on earth through the spiritual transformation of Christians, who would actively participate in progressive social change.

Although the Social Gospel and Progressive Movements contributed to several significant reforms in twentieth-century American society, capitalism continues to foster greed and militarism in the twenty-first century. Fortunately, there are *enlightened* capitalists and corporations that pragmatically and morally recognize the necessity for safe products, satisfied workers, and a safe environment. Nevertheless, there is much work to be done in our time to create an economic system that is worker-owned and democratically controlled, a cause championed by the Social Gospelers a century ago.

With the publication of *Christianity and the Social Crisis* (1907), Walter Rauschenbusch became the major spokesman for the Social Gospel Movement in the early twentieth century in the United States. Although it promoted social and economic change, at its heart the Social Gospel was a spiritual movement founded on the prayer of the Holy Spirit that seeks to "renew the face of the earth." That message remains as fresh and urgently needed as it was one hundred years ago.

As the Kingdom of God is the central doctrine for Rauschenbusch and the Social Gospel, that is the best place to begin our discussion of his work.

THE KINGDOM OF GOD

The Hebrew Prophets

Many biblical scholars in the early twentieth century (including Johannes Weiss, Albert Schweitzer, and Albert Ritschl), identified the Kingdom of God as the central theme in the preaching of Jesus. Rauschenbusch believed that Jesus's message of the Kingdom of God could only be properly understood in the context of the Hebrew prophets of the Old Testament. Rauschenbusch

held that the ministry of Jesus was a continuation and fulfill-
ment of the prophetic message that the Kingdom of God had
broken into history and was to play a key role in the transformation of that history in the here and now. Throughout most of
Hebraic history, the concept of the Kingdom of God as an other-
worldly heaven did not exist. Except for some vague references
to something that resembled an afterlife of hell or heaven, the
dominant teaching was that Yahweh's redeeming message was
to take place here on earth. God's salvation for the Jews was not
a salvation *from* this world, but rather a salvation *in and for* this
world. The words and actions—the life and death—of Jesus of
Nazareth tell us that he clearly stood in the tradition of the great
Jewish prophets.

Heaven and hell as destinations *after* this life came into Christianity in the early church period when Christian missionaries
mingled with religions and cultures that made a radical distinction between body and soul—as the Jews did not—and so
thought that the salvation of the soul could only be adequately
fulfilled when the soul left the body for an afterlife in heaven.
Hence, salvation gradually shifted away from a renewal of the
Garden on this earth to an abstract notion that heaven was
somewhere in the great beyond. Jesus quite clearly understood
the Reign of God in the prophetic sense and believed it would
take place in the historical reality of human beings, both flesh
and blood, matter and spirit.

Rauschenbusch discusses the key role the Jewish prophets played in the life of Jesus in the first chapter of his 1907
landmark work, *Christianity and the Social Crisis*. In a section
entitled "The Historical Roots of Christianity: The Hebrew
Prophets" Rauschenbusch writes, "The outcome of these first
historical chapters is that the essential purpose of Christianity
was to transform human society into the kingdom of God by
regenerating all human relations and reconstituting them in
accordance with the will of God." Rauschenbusch tells us that
early tribal religions focused not on morality but on ceremonial

methods of "placating the god, securing his gifts, and ascertaining his wishes." Hence, even immoral acts, such as "the immolation of human victims . . . the sacrifice of [a] woman's chastity . . . or the burning of the firstborn," could be acceptable as long as people pleased their gods. The Hebrew prophets denounced a religion that placed more emphasis on ritual worship than moral living. Rauschenbusch states, "Against this current conception of religion the prophets insisted on a right life as the true worship of God. . . . Morality to them was not merely a prerequisite of effective ceremonial worship. They brushed sacrificial ritual aside altogether as trifling compared with righteousness, nay, as a harmful substitute and a hindrance for ethical religion. 'I desire goodness and not sacrifice,' said Hosea (6:6), and Jesus was fond of quoting the words."

Jesus and the Kingdom of God

Rauschenbusch viewed the radical call to social justice in the great Jewish prophets—Amos, Isaiah, Micah, Jeremiah, Ezekiel, and Daniel—to be foundational to the saving mission of Jesus. Like the Jewish prophets of old, Jesus denounced the injustices of his day that resulted from the Roman military occupation of his homeland along with Jewish leaders who collaborated with the Romans in the oppression of their own people. Jesus championed the oppressed and downtrodden—the poor, women, Samaritans, the sick, the weak, lepers, the exploited, and the hopeless.

In Nazareth where he had been raised, Jesus announced his ministry with a quotation from the Hebrew prophet, Isaiah:

The spirit of the Lord is upon me, because he has anointed me to preach good news to the poor. He has sent me to proclaim release to the captives and recovery of sight to the blind, to set at liberty those who are oppressed, to proclaim the acceptable year of the Lord. (Luke 4:18–19)

Who were the "captives" and the "blind" and the "oppressed" in the time of Jesus? And, more importantly, who were their jailers and oppressors? The Jewish homeland was ruled by a foreign military power—the Romans—who taxed the people to death and beat them and imprisoned them at will. The Romans were assisted by some in the leadership of the Jews themselves, principally the Temple priests and some Sadducees and Scribes who profited by, or were silent during, the Roman occupation. The Romans and their Jewish collaborators were the oppressors in the time of Jesus. That is the political context in which Jesus began his ministry of liberation.

Like John the Baptist, Jesus denounced the leadership of his day as a "brood of vipers" for their oppression of the poor. Clearly, Jesus's mission was to liberate people from the oppressive religious, economic, and colonial despots who were destroying life for the Jewish people in Palestine. Hence, in parable after parable we find Jesus describing the Kingdom of God. In chapter 2 of *Christianity and the Social Crisis* Rauschenbusch tells us, "All the teaching of Jesus and all his thinking centered about the hope of the Kingdom of God."

Rauschenbusch's characteristics of the Kingdom of God are

1. *Love.* "The fundamental virtue in the ethics of Jesus was love."
2. *Nonviolence.* Jesus "would have nothing to do with bloodshed and violence."
3. *Universality.* Jesus rejected the old division of humanity into Jews and Gentiles in favor of the "Kingdom of God" that "became universal in scope, an affair of all humanity."
4. *Perils of Wealth.* The condemnation of riches in the teaching of Jesus is for Rauschenbusch central to the establishment of the Kingdom of God on earth. He stated, "The spirit of the world is always deluding men into thinking that 'a man's life consisteth in the abundance of the things

which he possesseth' (Luke 12:15), but when he builds
his life on that theory, he is lost to the kingdom of God."

Rauschenbusch held that the only prayer Jesus taught—the Our
Father—is central to his entire teaching on the Kingdom of God.
For Jesus does not tell us to look for the kingdom in an afterlife or in flight from the world, but rather here on earth. He
focuses on the words, "Thy kingdom come. Thy will be done, as
in heaven, so on earth." Rauschenbusch discusses the centrality
of the petition that God's Kingdom may come on earth: "There
is no request here that we be saved from earthliness and go to
heaven which has been the great object of churchly religion. We
pray here that heaven may be duplicated on earth through the
moral and spiritual transformation of humanity, both in its personal and its corporate life." This simple prayer is for Rauschenbusch the essence of the mission that Christians must undertake
to establish the Kingdom of God here on earth.

The Death of Jesus

We saw above that Jesus accepted his messianic mission in the
writings of Isaiah to "preach good news to the poor . . . to proclaim release to the captives . . . to give sight to the blind . . .
to set at liberty those who are oppressed . . . and to proclaim
the acceptable year of the Lord." Throughout his public ministry, he boldly and consistently proclaimed the Kingdom of God
on earth. During this time, he made many enemies principally
among those of the Jewish religious and political establishment
who not only mistook ritual for authentic religious ethics but
who also collaborated with the Roman occupation forces. It is
notable, therefore, that it is his *Jewish religious and political enemies* who call for his death and even more remarkable that they
call upon the hated Roman authorities to execute him.

The Gospel of Luke tells us that "the chief priests and captains
of the temple and elders who had come out against him" arose

and brought him before the Roman official Pontius Pilate, and they accused him of these crimes: "We have found this man perverting our nation, and forbidding us to give tribute to Caesar, and saying that he himself is Christ, a king" (Luke 22:52, 23:2). Anyone who told people not to pay taxes to the Romans and who claimed to be the king of the Jews would surely have raised grave concerns among the Roman authorities who forced the Jews to pay tax to Rome and held that only Caesar was the king of all lands. Hence, quite clearly Jesus was killed for political crimes against the Roman Empire. The form of punishment—crucifixion—was reserved for the worst of crimes: treason and seditious or revolutionary activity against the empire. Hence, the death of Jesus is plainly consistent with what he spent his life doing: preaching the Kingdom of God in his own country in his own time for his own people. This meant refusal to cooperate with Rome, including the payment of taxes and, most important, recognizing the Jewish Kingdom of God rather than the kingdom of the Roman Caesar Augustus who was called *Divi Filius*—Son of God.

Jesus began his public ministry with the proclamation of prophetic political and ethical ideals and was executed by the Romans for these very same political and ethical crimes. A great deal of research on the historical and political context of the New Testament conducted in the twentieth century examines the economic and political nature of the mission of Jesus. (See especially John Dominic Crossan's *Jesus: A Revolutionary Biography* [1994] and Walter Wink's books, including, *Jesus and Nonviolence: A Third Way* [2003], among many works that focus on the nonviolent revolution of Jesus.)

The eventual abandonment by the Christian church of the revolutionary Jesus led church teaching to focus on the nonpolitical message of personal salvation that took place in an afterlife. In their 1892 statement on the Brotherhood of the Kingdom, Rauschenbusch and fellow Baptist ministers Nathaniel Schmidt and

Leighton Williams accuse the church of abandoning the idea of a political and economic Kingdom of God here on earth in favor of an individualistic and other-worldly notion of salvation. We read in the brotherhood statement:

> Because the Kingdom of God has been dropped as the primary and comprehensive aim of Christianity, and personal salvation has been substituted for it, therefore men seek to save their own souls and are selfishly indifferent to the evangelization of the world. Because the individualist conception of personal salvation has pushed out of sight the collective idea of a Kingdom of God on earth, Christian men seek for the salvation of individuals and are comparatively indifferent to the spread of the spirit of Christ in the political, industrial, social scientific, and artistic life of humanity, and have left these as the undisturbed possessions of the spirit of the world. Because the Kingdom of God has been understood as a state to be inherited in a future life rather than as something to be realized here and now, therefore Christians have been contented with a low plane of life here and have postponed holiness to the future.

Tragically, so much in this statement continues to be true of all too many followers of Jesus in the twenty-first century.

MAJOR INFLUENCES

It is said that we all stand on the shoulders of those who went before us. Rauschenbusch was blessed to have a wide range of pastoral experiences and intellectual mentors in his life who contributed mightily to his teaching on the revolutionary nature of the Kingdom of God. The following are significant influences on the formation of Rauschenbusch's spirituality and intellectual development.

Baptist Faith

Rauschenbusch's father, August (1816–1899), emigrated from Germany to the United States in 1846 as a Lutheran minister in the Pietist tradition. He was impressed, however, by Anabaptist spirituality and theology, and came to believe that the Baptist Church was closer to the New Testament ideal both in its ethical ideals and church governance. August became a Baptist minister and this conversion had a major impact on his young son, Walter.

In 1912 Rauschenbusch published a series of sermons entitled, "Why I Am a Baptist" in *The Baptist Commonwealth*. He endorsed the Anabaptist tradition of adult conversion to Christianity, and he believed the Anabaptists represented a more thorough reform in Christianity than that of the Lutheran and Calvinist Churches. He offered four reasons for his Baptist convictions:

1. It is necessary to have a personal experience of Jesus;
2. Baptist churches are Christian democracies;
3. Baptist worship is centered on living a Christ-like life. In his words, "A loving and pure life is the true liturgy of Christian worship"; and
4. Baptists have no fixed creed or set of doctrines. He states, "It seems to me a great thing that Baptists are not chained by creeds, but have taken the Bible as their authority."

But Rauschenbusch was no biblical fundamentalist, since he strongly supported the role of historical research and the social sciences in his understanding of his religious convictions.

Theological and Philosophical Influences

Beginning with the influence of his German-born father, Augustus, and extending through his undergraduate years in a German Gymnasium (1883–1886) along with sabbaticals in Germany and England (1891), Rauschenbusch was exposed to the latest research on theology, scripture, history, and the social sciences that dominated the German research universities of the nineteenth century. Among the most important influence on Rauschenbusch was the work of the famous professor of dogmatic theology and ethics at the University of Gottingen, Albrecht Ritschl (1822–1899). Ritschl understood Christianity primarily to be an ethical religion (in contrast to a religion based on doctrine, or one defined by ritual). Ritschl's core teaching was that Jesus taught us to establish the Kingdom of God here on earth.

In his quest to find a concrete expression of the Reign of God in people's lives, Rauschenbusch traveled several times to Great Britain to study British socialism and the tradition of worker cooperatives. He was influenced by the work of the Welsh manufacturer Robert Owen (1771–1858) and the Rochdale Pioneers who elaborated Owen's ideas of utopian socialism. He was further influenced by Charles Kingsley (1819–1875), a priest in the Church of England and a Christian Socialist who championed Bible politics or politics according to the Kingdom of God.

American Influences

Although Walter Rauschenbusch became the most prominent of the American Social Gospelers, the Social Gospel began principally with Josiah Strong and Washington Gladden. A Congregationalist minister, Josiah Strong (1847–1916), had an optimistic view of human nature and believed that the Kingdom of God could become a reality on earth. He believed that the central teaching of Jesus was the Kingdom of God and that selfishness could be overcome by science, cooperative action, and the power of love. Another Congregationalist, Washington Gladden (1836–1918) contributed mightily to Rauschenbusch's thought. Gladden believed that love was a social force that could remake the face of the earth, and he was one of the first Protestants to support labor unions. He believed that the Kingdom of God was bigger than the church and that the church's primary mission was to serve the kingdom in history.

Another important influence came from the political economist Henry George (1839–1897), whose book *Progress and Poverty* (1879) decried the enormous profits that rich people were making from their ownership of property that was not acquired through work. He was especially incensed at the rich landlords who owned blocks of crowded and unsanitary tenements and reaped the profits from exploited workers who worked ten- to twelve-hour workdays, six days a week. George's solution—a *single tax* on the rich that was to be used to benefit the poor—became a rallying cry of the socialists of the day. George believed that unearned income on the part of the wealthy through exploitation of the poor was parasitic and contrary to the Gospel. Rauschenbusch's view of economics and politics was profoundly influenced by George. He wrote in 1912 in *Christianizing the Social Order*, "I owe my own first awakening to the world of social problems to the agitation of Henry George in 1886, and wish here to record my lifelong debt to this single-minded apostle of a great truth."

Another strong influence on Rauschenbusch during his Hell's Kitchen days was a Catholic priest, Fr. Edward McGlynn (1837–1900). McGlynn publicly supported George and paid a heavy price with his archbishop for his involvement in the struggle for worker justice and the rights of the poor. In 1887 Rauschenbusch attended a speech by McGlynn that closed with the words, "Thy kingdom come. Thy will be done on earth." Rauschenbusch was deeply moved by McGlynn and made this quote from the Our Father his own as the years went on. (See "The Social Meaning of the Lord's Prayer" in Chapter 6 of this volume for a more complete discussion of Rauschenbusch's convictions.)

Hell's Kitchen

Perhaps the most important influence on Rauschenbusch's thought was his experience as a Baptist pastor on the west side

of New York City called Hell's Kitchen (1886–1897). His experience with the exploitation of the poor by rich landlords and
the robber barons of the day radicalized him for the rest of his
life. He witnessed poverty, disease, unsanitary and crowded tenements, long working hours, poor food, inadequate hospitals,
child labor, and the exploitation of women, which characterized
"The Gilded Age." These were the special ravages of capitalism.
He came almost to despise the rich because of their callousness
and exploitation of the poor masses.

It was during this time that the Kingdom of God on earth
became the dominant mission for the rest of his life. He was
especially troubled by the large number of funerals he conducted
for children, and understood them to be the special victims of
an economic system that exploited people and nature itself in
the pursuit of greed. Through his studies and travels and the
influence of Henry George he came to realize that there was
another way to organize economics and that was the way of
socialism. Although he strongly supported democratic socialism
(he did not believe in state ownership of the means of production), Rauschenbusch did not equate any specific economic or
political system with the Kingdom of God since he regarded the
kingdom as "always but coming."

THE INFLUENCE OF THE SOCIAL GOSPEL

While others laid the foundation of the Social Gospel, undoubt-
edly it was Walter Rauschenbusch who became its most prominent spokesman. With his publication, in 1907, of *Christianity
and the Social Crisis,* Rauschenbusch achieved instant fame,
and his name quickly came to be associated with the impact of
the Social Gospel on American society. The book quickly sold
50,000 copies, an enormous number for that time. His popular book on *Prayers of the Social Awakening,* in 1910, added
a personal and spiritual dimension to his thought, and his final
book, in 1918, *A Theology for the Social Gospel,* added some
theological depth to the Social Gospel, especially in answering

critics that he did not sufficiently account for the reality of sin in the world. Rauschenbusch focused primarily on what he called institutional sinfulness that was practiced especially by the capitalists of his day and by the corporations they created, which exploited poor workers in order to maximize profit.

Rauschenbusch's earliest influence was on his own church. Beginning in 1892 when he formed the Brotherhood of the Kingdom in Hell's Kitchen in New York City, and later when he served as professor at Rochester Theological Seminary (NY), Rauschenbusch influenced many new pastors to espouse the Social Gospel in their sermons and pastoral activity. People began supporting the movement to end child labor, to support women's suffrage, and to pursue the notion of a democratic workplace where workers would own and control the means of production. Communism and socialism were already having an impact on American society, but the Social Gospel added a religious dimension that also served as a corrective to some who advocated violence in the creation of a more just society.

The heyday of the Social Gospel began in the 1890s and started to decline after 1917 when patriotic fervor for the Great War (WWI) in the United States stifled criticism of capitalism and militarism. Socialists like Eugene V. Debs were imprisoned and the infamous post-WWI Palmer raids fueled the great *Red Scare*, resulting in the deportation and imprisonment of many innocent people. Widely criticized for his refusal to condemn Germany in WWI, Rauschenbusch's invitations to speak melted away. With the turn to biblical fundamentalism on the part of many Protestants in the 1920s and the accompanying withdrawal from politics and social criticism, the Social Gospel suffered a further decline. Nevertheless, the formation of the Protestant Federal Council of Churches after WWI and the continuation of Social Gospel education in seminaries and universities continued to spread its influence. Many ideas that originated in the Social Gospel and the Progressive Era found themselves in FDR's New Deal and other governmental programs.

Perhaps the most serious challenge to the Social Gospel came from one of its own, Reinhold Niebuhr (1892–1971). As a young Lutheran pastor in Detroit, Niebuhr was inspired by Social Gospel theology to criticize the rampant capitalism of Henry Ford and other abuses of his day. Niebuhr, however, was profoundly influenced by his Lutheran theology that held to the Augustinian doctrine of Original Sin. This doctrine taught that sin had devastating effects on each human being, since it was biologically transmitted from parent to child. Many taught that children who died without baptism would go to hell. The Original Sin in each of us characterized our lives and history; humanity was seen, in the words of Augustine of Hippo (354–430), as a *massa damnata* (doomed mass). In this light, the Kingdom of God here on earth was, therefore, clearly an impossibility, and those who proclaimed such an ideal were foolish optimists and dreamers. Reinhold Niebuhr accepted the Augustinian distinction between the sinful City of Man here on earth and the beatific City of God that existed in a heaven after death. His most famous work on this subject, the two-volume *The Nature and Destiny of Man*, was published as the storm clouds of World War II were forming over Europe.

Niebuhr's thought came to be known as "Christian Realism" and it effectively ended the influence of the Social Gospel, practically down to our own time. Niebuhr was also influenced by the Great Depression and the rise of Adolf Hitler and the spread of fascism around the world. He adopted a theology of paradox and was fond of pointing out the irony of history. He held that progress was inevitably accompanied by the seeds of its own destruction and that life here on earth could not follow any hope for the Kingdom of God, such as Rauschenbusch preached. In the 1930s Niebuhr abandoned his early pacifism and socialism and muted his critique of capitalism and militarism. After World War II he was strongly anticommunist and argued against the possibility of world government. Capitalist champion Henry Luce put Niebuhr's picture on the cover of *Time* magazine in

1948 with the caption "Man's Story Is Not a Success Story."
Reinhold Niebuhr's famed theological realism was in fact a
return to the early fifth-century theological pessimism of Augustine of Hippo that abandoned any hope for the Reign of God
here on earth. Just as Augustine in his condemnation of Pelagian
theology in the early fifth century cast a long dark shadow on
Gospel-based Christian ethics, so Niebuhr caused many to reject
the Social Gospel.

Despite these setbacks, the Social Gospel nevertheless contributed to the New Deal and other progressive governmental
programs in the United States and Canada in the 1930s and
1940s, continuing to our own time.

Perhaps the most famous person that Rauschenbusch influenced was Martin Luther King Jr. (1929–1968). His first
encounter with the thought of Rauschenbusch came at More-
house College and Crozer Theological Seminary—both Baptist
schools. He studied Rauschenbusch more seriously under Dr.
Walter Muelder when he enrolled for his PhD at Boston University. Rauschenbusch's influence on Dr. King was profound and
had a major influence on his attitude toward capitalism, labor
unions, and, of course, political activity. In *Stride toward Freedom* (1958), Dr. King stated,

> Rauschenbusch had done a great service for the Chris-
> tian Church by insisting the gospel deals with the whole
> man, not only his soul but his body; not only his spiri-
> tual well-being but his material well-being. It has been
> my conviction that ever since reading Rauschenbusch
> that any religion which professes to be concerned about
> the soul of men and is not concerned about the social
> and economic conditions that scar that soul, is a spiritu-
> ally moribund religion waiting for the day to be buried.

Many of the ministers and political leaders who were involved
in the Civil Rights Movement were inspired by the Social Gospel Movement. Today the Social Gospel Movement is routinely

taught in many Protestant and some Roman Catholic schools of theology and continues to have a determinative influence in the field of Christian Social Ethics.

While it would take a book in itself to document all the scholars and activists that the Social Gospel influenced in the past one hundred years, just one other follower of Rauschenbusch deserves mention. Tommy Douglas (1904–1986) was a Baptist minister from Canada who, as Premier of Saskatchewan, introduced Canada's single-payer, universal health care program among many other progressive reforms. Douglas became steeped in Rauschenbusch's theology while in seminary, and it became the blueprint of his life in government service. Douglas spent his entire life dedicated to the cause of social justice and helping the poor. He is but one of many *students* of Rauschenbusch who took seriously the challenge to establish the Kingdom of God on earth.

The list is quite long of people who were influenced by Rauschenbusch. It includes Jane Addams, William Barber, John C. Bennett, Paul Deats, Richard Deats, Gary Dorrien, Tommy Douglas, Harry Emerson Fosdick, Mohandas Gandhi, Martin Luther King Jr., George McGovern, Walter Muelder, A. J. Muste, the young Reinhold Niebuhr, Vida Scutter, Ronald H. Sider, Max Stackhouse, Glenn Stassen, Desmond Tutu, William A. Visser t'Hooft, Jim Wallis, Rabbi Stephen Wise, and Cornell West.

The reader will note the sad lack of more women's names on this list other than Jane Addams and Vida Scutter. This is in part due to the historical fact that women were rarely involved either as ordained ministers or professional theologians at the turn of the twentieth century. But, of course, women were involved in many aspects of the wider Progressive Movement that included the right of women to vote, the promotion of civil rights, settlement houses for the poor, social work, education, and anti-war activism. An important volume that documents the role that women played in social justice activities at the time of the Social Gospel and after is the very fine work edited by Wendy J.

Deichmann Edwards and Carolyn De Swarte Gifford entitled, *Gender and the Social Gospel* (2003). Although not formally associated with the Social Gospel many of the women in this book engaged in much the same prophetic activity but with far little notice by (male) historians and journalists at that time.

RAUSCHENBUSCH AND CATHOLICISM

In the second chapter of *Christianity and the Social Crisis* Rauschenbusch discusses how the Christian church abandoned the Kingdom of God as its primary mission on earth. In his references to the *Christian* church after the second century, he refers to what was to become the Roman Catholic Church. In the chapter entitled "Why Has Christianity Never Undertaken the Work of Social Reconstruction?" Rauschenbusch discusses the salient reasons why the church did not live up to its revolutionary potential. These reasons include the persecution of the early church, Neo-Platonic dualism (radical division between body and soul), ascetic (other-worldly) piety, monasticism (flight from the world), theological pessimism (Original Sin), clerical celibacy (sexual intimacy detracts from spirituality), emphasis on ritual over ethics, dogmatism, identification of the Kingdom of God with the church, subservience to the state, the disappearance of democracy in the church, and the condemnation of rational inquiry and science.

Since many of these elements are historically found in the Catholic Church, some authors have cast Rauschenbusch as anti-Catholic and, indeed, anti-Catholicism was rampant in nineteenth- and early twentieth-century America. A careful reading of Rauschenbusch reveals, however, that he simply was objectively examining why the church either withdrew from the world or identified with the state to the detriment of the Gospel. In addition, Rauschenbusch respected Fr. Edward McGlynn (a Catholic priest of the Archdiocese of New York) and often quoted him. Rauschenbsch's writings also reveal a high deal of respect for St. Francis of Assisi and the Jesuits. (As a young pastor in Hell's Kitchen he formed his own *Society of Jesus* based on Ignatian spirituality.) Nevertheless, there was a good deal of hostility on the part of Protestants to Catholics in nineteenth- and early twentieth-century America, and some of Rauschenbusch's rhetoric reflected that animus. Ecumenism as we know it today was condemned by both sides, and Catholic speakers were forbidden even to appear on the same stage as Protestants.

It is remarkable, therefore, to note that while the Protestant Social Gospel was in its heyday, there was a simultaneous surge in Roman Catholic teaching on social justice. In Germany, Bishop Wilhelm Emmanuel von Kettler (1811–1877), a champion of the working class and critic of capitalism, had a strong influence on the publication of *Rerum Novarum* (On the Condition of the Working Classes), Pope Leo XIII's groundbreaking encyclical letter of 1891. In this letter Pope Leo strongly criticized capitalism and *encouraged* the formation of labor unions and other measures to assist workers and the poor. In the United States, Fr. John A. Ryan (1869–1945) published *A Living Wage: Its Ethical and Economic Aspects* (1906, with an introduction by Rauschenbusch's friend Richard T. Ely). Ryan was the author in 1919 of the influential "Bishops' Program of Social Reconstruction" that put the Roman Catholic bishops on the record for far-reaching economic reforms, including the abolition of monopolies, support for labor unions, equal pay for women, a guaranteed living wage, and state-provided social insurance for "illness, invalidity, unemployment, and old age," among many other reform proposals. Many of these visionary proposals found their way into FDR's New Deal in the 1930s.

Unfortunately, however, although working for similar social and economic goals, it seems that Protestants and Catholics hardly talked to each other. Many Protestants were still adamantly anti-Catholic, and many Catholics viewed with disdain the Protestant *heretics* who had abandoned what they considered the true church of Christ.

Rauschenbusch would be amazed, therefore, to witness the global ecumenical movement that developed during the 1950s and 1960s between Catholics and Protestants along with interreligious dialogue with Jews, Muslims, Buddhists, and other faith traditions. Numerous official Catholic statements have reflected what we might call a Catholic Social Gospel. These include Pope John XXIII, *Pacem in Terris* (Peace on Earth, 1963), Vatican II's *Gaudium et Spes* (The Church in the Modern World, 1965), the World Synod of Bishops' "Justice in the World" (1971), and the U.S. Bishops' pastoral letter "Economic Justice for All" (1986). In addition, the advent of Liberation Theology that began in Latin America with the publication of Gustavo Gutiérrez's *A Theology of Liberation: History, Politics, and Salvation* (1973), contributed mightily to a focus in Catholic theology on a New Testament–based call to pursue the Reign of God in history.

CONCLUSION

Rauschenbusch and other Social Gospelers would be quite pleased at the progress that humankind has made since the 1890s. Child labor has been abolished, women have the right to vote, people of color and workers have (some) legal protection, and there exists today a middle class that did not exist in their time. Of course, this progress is due only in part to the efforts of the Social Gospel; but to the extent that religious leaders played a role in promoting social progress, they do deserve a good deal of credit.

However, despite these gains—and they are real gains often achieved against great odds—they remain more cosmetic than substantive. Capitalism remains an economic system that is founded on greed and the utilitarian philosophy that the end justifies the means. Millions adhere to the religion of capitalism, although they will never share in the wealth they create for the ruling 1 percent. Capitalism and militarism continue to dominate much of the world's economy and the welfare and rights of our environment, of animals, and workers are perpetually in danger of being violated in the name of profit for the very few. And, saddest of all, it is often the poorest and most oppressed who help elect politicians who despise them and use them only for their own gain. To that extent things have not changed much since the 1890s.

But there is hope. Many of us of an older generation thought that the word socialist had practically been banned from the English language, especially in the United States. It is remarkable, therefore, that so many politicians are openly calling themselves democratic socialists and winning elections in the United States, the last great bastion of capitalism. There is hope today also since some Protestant and Catholic Christian churches have accepted the Kingdom of God here on earth as the central focus of their mission. The finest pages of human history have yet to be written. Our best days lie ahead.

RECOMMENDED READINGS

For those wishing to understand the Social Gospel and Rauschenbusch's message, there is no better place to begin than one of the Synoptic Gospels: Matthew, Mark, or Luke. Take your time and meditate on the Good News that Jesus came to preach among us. You will see how much he was consumed with the Kingdom of God; almost all of his sermons and stories (parables) deal in some fashion with how God's Reign must take place on earth. Pay especial attention to the relationship between Jesus and his political enemies. Focus on why he was put to death and you will understand how the message of the Kingdom of God challenged the corrupt leaders of his time—and of our own.

Following are just a few of the many fine books that have been written about Rauschenbusch and the Social Gospel.

William H. Brackney, General Editor (2018). *Walter Rauschenbusch: Published Works and Selected Writings in Three*

Volumes. This three-volume work cannot be recommended too highly. It contains just about all of Rauschenbusch's writings, including his books. Especially recommended are William H. Brackney's introductions to Rauschenbusch's historical origins and theological thinking in Volumes I and III and David P. Gushee's introduction to Walter Rauschenbusch's ethics in Volume II. There is also an extensive bibliography of works by and about Rauschenbusch in Volume III that is highly valuable to the reader who may want to pursue further studies in Rauschenbusch.

Gary Dorrien (2003). *The Making of American Liberal Theology: Idealism, Realism, and Modernity.*

Wendy J. Deichmann Edwards and Carolyn De Swarte Gifford (2003). *Gender and the Social Gospel.*

Christopher H. Evans (2004). *The Kingdom Is Always but Coming: A Life of Walter Rauschenbusch.*

Christopher H. Evans (2017). *The Social Gospel in American Religion: A History.*

Winthrop H. Hudson (1984). *Walter Rauschenbusch: Selected Writings.*

A NOTE ON LANGUAGE

Readers of this book will, of course, note that so much of the language used in Rauschenbusch's writings, as well as in this introduction, is what today we would call sexist or noninclusive language. The Kingdom of God should be the Reign of God, and it is interesting to note that even Rauschenbusch occasionally used the term *Reign of God* in his own lifetime. Concern for faithfulness to the historical record, however, requires that the author's original language be used. We would like to think that if Rauschenbusch were among us today, he would use inclusive language, and that would have been consistent with the liberating message he preached in his own time.

1

Beneath the Glitter

This short passage was written in 1887 when Rauschenbusch was a young Baptist pastor in the Hell's Kitchen section of New York City. He invites the reader to look beyond the glitter of the city in order to see the suffering of the people who are the victims of capitalism. His work among poor and exploited workers and their families was foundational to his embracing the Social Gospel. Published in the Christian Enquirer, New York.

Why, yes, it is a pleasant evening. Out to see life in New York City, eh? Well, Saturday night is a good time to see it on this avenue. Lots of people. Hold on there! That fellow nearly took my hat off. Rather interrupts conversation to squeeze through and dodge around.

Fine sight, you think? Yes, the stores are bright, people well-dressed mostly; they all look busy and happy, as they push by. Got to do their shopping for Sunday, you know, and their love-making for all the week. The world is not so bad a world as some would like to make it. That's your verdict, is it, from what you see? You'll go and pooh-pooh this talk about want and degradation and the iron law, and all that. Well, go ahead, you'll only be one of a crowd who know the family because they've looked at the front door, and say the elephant is a tree, because they stumbled against his leg getting made, am I? Oh no, only a bit wild. You'd do the same if you had eyes to see.

There, do you see that big clothing house on the corner there? Brilliantly lighted; show windows gorgeous; all hum and happiness. But somewhere in that big house there's a little bullet-headed tailor doubled up over the coat he is to alter, and as surely as I know that my hand is pressing your arm, I know too that he is choking down the sobs and trying to keep the water out of his eyes. Why? Because his little girl is going to die tonight and he can't be there. Consumption, pulmonary. Been wasting away for months, can't sleep except her head is on his breast. And then he can't sleep when her panting is in his ears. He has just been draining his life to sustain hers, and yet Minnie is all the world to him. She's the only drop of sweetness in his cup; all the rest is gall. Hard work; nothing to look forward to; wife grown bitter and snarling; and tonight the girl dies. How do I know? Just been there. Her forehead is getting clammy and her whole body rocks with the effort to get breath. She's whispering, "Tell my papa to come," but he'll not be there before one o'clock tonight. Saturday night, you know; very busy; sorry, but can't spare him. O yes, you can say that: ought to go home, permission or none; but that means throwing up a job that he has been hanging to by his finger nails. It will be six months before he gets another. And so he has to sew away and let his little girl die three blocks off. When he gets home he can sob over her corpse; what more does he want? Exceptional case, you think. Not a bit of it. It's the drop on the crest of the wave, but there are a million other drops underneath it, all hurled along, or that one drop wouldn't be so high.

Do you see that old woman with the basket just turned into the street? Yes, the little one with the shawl over her head. Well, that is one of the meekest souls in this city. She and her husband live in two little rooms in a rear house. They pay about the lowest rent I have found in this neighborhood, $6 a month. He earns from $1.50 to $3.00 per week, so you can figure how much they live on. Lazy? No, sir! They have just toiled and toiled all their lives. She has kept house and borne children and washed and scrubbed and saved. Why aren't they better off, you ask? That's what I want you to tell me. Here are these two old people standing at the close of a life of work and frugality, and watching old age and helplessness creeping down on them. And what have they got to face it with? A bit of bare furniture; one son who drank and has drifted out of their sight; another son a barber, who just scrapes together enough to feed and clothe his family while they live and to pay off their funeral expenses after they die; a few graves across the river; a hope in heaven, and $70 in the savings bank. Ah, you say, that's something. Yes, it is something, more than I've got; but no soul knows how they stinted to get that much, and what an anchor of hope that little sum is for the coming years. And they gave me a dollar "for the heathen" the other day. Case for charity you say. Yes, daub your walls with mortar to fill up the cracks; but what makes the wall split up so, anyway?

Do you see that girl in front of . . . got to go, eh? Bored you, didn't I? Yes, guess I am something of a crank on these things. Wish you'd trot around with me for a week; you wouldn't think so highly of things as they are. Good night, my boy.

2

Christianity Revolutionary

Rauschenbusch began writing Christianity Revolutionary *in 1891–1892 while on a study leave in Germany. Although it was not published in his lifetime, it did serve as the basis of many of his writings, especially his most famous work,* Christianity and the Social Crisis *(1907). It was published for the first time by Max Stackhouse in 1968 under the title,* The Righteousness of the Kingdom. *The following are the first two chapters of this work.*

CHRISTIANITY IS BY ITS NATURE REVOLUTIONARY

Its revolutionary character is apparent from the spiritual ancestry to which it traces its lineage. Jesus was the successor of the Old Testament prophets. The common people of his day discerned this kinship and whispered that he must be Elijah or Jeremiah or some other of the prophets (Mt. 16, 4). He himself repeatedly drew the parallel between the work and lot of the prophets and his own. Like the prophets he was rejected in his own country (Mt. 13, 57). Like the prophets he was to suffer at the hands of the wicked husbandmen (Lk. 20, 4–18). Like all the prophets he must perish at Jerusalem (Lk. 13, 34–35). His forerunner he calls a prophet, a second Elijah (Mk. 9, 11–13; Lk. 7, 26); and to his followers he predicts that like the prophets they

26

will be slandered and persecuted (Mt. 5, 10–12), and at last like
the prophets meet their death (Mt. 23, 29–36).

Now what were these prophets, to whose spirit and purpose
Jesus felt so close a kinship, and whose lot he expected to share?
The prophets were the revolutionists of their age. They were
dreamers of Utopias. They pictured an ideal state of society in
which the poor should be judged with equity and the cry of
the oppressed should no longer be heard; a time in which men
would beat their idle swords into ploughshares and their spears
into pruning hooks, for then the nations would learn war no
more (Is. 2, 4). No slight amelioration contented them; nothing but a change so radical that they dared to represent it as a
repealing of the ancient and hallowed covenant and the con-
struction of a new one. A proposal to abolish the Constitution
of the United States would not seem so revolutionary to us as
this proposal must have seemed to the contemporaries of the
prophets.

They did not expect such a change to glide in without a struggle. A day of vengeance would have to precede it. It would be
like a refiner's fire and like fillers' soap (Mal. 3, 2). The Lord
would have a reckoning with those that oppressed the hireling in
his wages, the widow, and the fatherless, and those that turned
aside the stranger from his right (Mal. 3, 5). He would come
upon the high ones and the kings of the earth, and gather them
as prisoners are gathered in the dungeon, and shut them up in
prison (Is. 24, 21–22). For they had eaten up the vineyard; the
spoil of the poor was in their houses; they had beaten God's
people to pieces; they had ground the faces of the poor (Is. 3,
13–15).

Nor were the prophets mere impractical dreamers and
declaimers. They were men of action. They overthrew dynas-
ties. They were popular agitators, tribunes of the people. They
rebuked to their faces kings who had taken the plain man of his
wife or tricked him out of his ancestral holding.

These were the men whose successor Christ professed to be. This does not imply that he sanctioned all their actions or proposed to copy all their methods. But it does imply that of all the forces in the national history of Israel the prophets were the most worthy of his approval and most akin to his spirit.

But the prophets were the revolutionary element in Israel. The revolutionary character of Christ's work appears also from the elements in contemporary life to which he allied himself.

The Messianic hope, kindled and fanned by the prophets, was still glowing in the hearts of the people. When John the Baptist lifted up his voice by the Jordan, men were on the alert immediately, querying "whether haply he were the Messiah" (Lk. 3, 15). The atmosphere of Palestine was surcharged with this electricity. When, in the synagogue at Nazareth, Jesus chose for his text that passage of Isaiah which tells of glad tidings to the poor, of release to the captives, of liberty to the bruised, and of the acceptable year of the Lord, "the eyes of all in the synagogue were fastened upon him." The passage was universally understood to refer to the Messianic era. They were breathlessly eager to hear what attitude he would assume. And what was his attitude? He told them the time had now come: "To-day hath this scripture been fulfilled in your ears" (Lk. 4, 16–21).

It is plain that the people counted him as their own. They were waiting to see him raise the standard of revolt and were ready to follow him as their king (Jo. 6, 14–15). And in spite of all apparent disappointments to which he subjected them, they had their eye on him still. When at the very end he entered Jerusalem with something of public state, all their hopes revived and they hailed him as the Messiah coming to claim the Kingdom of his father David.

It is true that Christ steadfastly refused to fulfill their expectations. We shall discuss later on his reasons for doing so. Yet the fact remains that he did appeal to the Messianic hope. He found his followers among those in whom that hope was liveliest. He came so near to fulfilling the people's idea of the Messiah that they were always on the verge of expectation. To the Sadducean enemies of the Messianic movement he seemed, even at the end of his ministry, so closely connected with the movement that they regarded it as only a question of time when he would lead the revolt and plunge the nation into war with Rome (John 11, 47–50).

The contents of the Messianic hope of course varied. With some it was dyed in blood, with others it was irradiated by heaven. But this element was common to all who entertained it: they were weary of present conditions; they were longing for a radically different state of affairs; and they were sure that it would come and were ready to help it on. In other words, the Messianic hope was a revolutionary hope.

That this revolutionary element existed even among the most spiritually minded men and women is discernible from the recorded words of those choice souls among whom Jesus, by God's own appointment, spent his early years and by whom his thoughts were moulded. The hymns in the first two chapters of Luke, judged by internal evidence, express the Messianic hope before it had been modified by the teachings and the life of Jesus. Note the revolutionary tone:

> He hath shewed strength with his arm;
> He hath scattered the proud in the imagination of their
>   heart.
> He hath put down princes from their thrones
> And hath exalted them of low degree.
> The hungry he hath filled with good things;
> And the rich he hath sent empty away." (Lk. 1, 51–53)

Those were the thoughts of her whose blood ran in the veins of Jesus and who had the fashioning of his early years. Zacharias blesses Jehovah for having raised up a horn of salvation,

> Salvation from our enemies, and from the hand of all
>   that hate us;
> . . . That he would grant unto us,
> That we, being delivered out of the hands of our ene-
>   mies
> Should serve him without fear
> In holiness and righteousness before him all our days.
>   (Lk. 1, 71, 74, 75)

In these two songs the thought of the Messianic victory pre-
dominates, and Simeon thinks more of the conflict which shall
precede it and which will bring about the prostration of some
and the elevation of others: "Behold this child is set for the
falling and the rising of many in Israel; and for a sign which
is spoken against; yea and a sword shall pierce through thine
own soul; that thoughts out of many hearts may be revealed"
(Lk. 2, 34–35). But in them all is the prophetic hope: a mighty
uprising of Jehovah, a casting down of the powerful and wicked,
and then peace and prosperity for the poor and righteous. And
when finally we turn to the man whom Jesus himself has called
the choicest fruit of the all past, we find the same revolutionary
language.

> Make ye ready the way of the Lord!
> Make his paths straight!
> Every valley shall be
> And every mountain and hill shall be brought low;
> And the crooked shall become straight,
> And the rough way smooth.

Here is a general straightening out and leveling as a prepa-
ration for the coming of the Messiah. His advice to the people explains what he meant by straightening out the crooked
ways and razing the high places: "He that hath two coats let him

impart to him that hath none; and he that hath food let him do likewise." The abolition of social inequality, according to John, was the first step in the Messianic renewal. His conception of the Messiah's work is likewise expressed in flaming images of destruction and overthrowing: a dusty threshing-floor, a sifting of wheat and chaff, a consuming fire, a crashing down of rotten trees. The baptism of John, in which his preaching found its dramatic expression, was a revolutionary symbol. It was the baptism of repentance; a turning away from old ways and a consecration to the new; it was the rite of initiation into "the remnant," which would be prepared for the coming of the Messiah and fit for the new order of things to be ushered in by the Messianic judgment.

The revolutionary character of his work is expressly asserted by Christ.

He came to cast fire upon the earth, and he longed to see it kindled. He had come to hide a leaven in the world's trough of meal, and it would be in a ferment until the leaven had done its work.

He brought a new spirit and the new spirit would demand new forms of life. Men then as now had small discernment for the new spirit, but they raised a decided protest against the abolition of old forms and the evolution of new ones. He might bring new wine, if he wished, but let him put it in the old vessels. But Jesus told them that they must not think that his young, bubbling wine could be bottled up in the old cracked wine-skins, or that it would not suffice him reverently to patch bits of new cloth on the most shameless rents of the tattered garment wherewith society was seeking to cover its nakedness. A new spirit plus new forms and customs and institutions; that means revolution.

The change he was inaugurating was so radical, that after its consummation it would be found that the first had become last and the last first. Ideas now dominant would then be smiled over. Institutions now regarded as existing, *jure divino*, would then be recognized as having existed *jure diabolico*. Men now on top in society and state and church, would go to the bottom, and many now despised and neglected would then be honored and would reign over the tribes of Israel. Such a reversal of values presupposes sweeping changes in the general conceptions and judgments prevalent in human society, and necessarily also in the social and political institutions in which these conceptions and judgments find their embodiment.

Jesus knew very well the difficulties of the work he had undertaken. He knew that those who have seats at the banquet where the old wine is served have little taste for the new. He knew that those who hold the places of power and privilege will seldom resign them without a struggle. He foresaw a terrible conflict, a division of humanity into hostile camps. A man would be set at variance with his father, and a daughter with her mother. Two in a household would be ranged against the other three. The strongest ties in the world would snap when they encountered this new force.

Jesus foresaw all this. If ever a heart was tender, surely it was his. Yet he did not shrink from precipitating the world into such a conflict. His was the revolutionary spirit, loving and inflexible.

Moreover his attitude became more revolutionary as he went on; his language grew sterner, his opposition to the powers that were, more unyielding, until it grew plain that the most moral community of that age, and perhaps the most religious society of any age, was engaged in irreconcilable conflict with Jesus Christ; a conflict which could end only with the overthrow of one of the conflicting forces. We know that it did end with the apparent overthrow of the one and the actual overthrow of the other.

This interpretation of the tendency of Christ's work is borne out by the attitude of his contemporaries. Those who had anything to gain by a change, followed him and heard him gladly. Those who had anything to lose by a change, feared him. They feared him enough to hate him. They hated him enough to kill him. Self-interest is short-sighted, but its sight is marvelously keen for all that comes within the range of its vision. When the chief priests and scribes and elders, the dignitaries of society as it then existed, combined to put him down at all hazard, they were not stabbing at shadows. They were closing with a deadly foe and they knew it. It was either his life or their privileges. They had no mind to be placed at the bottom in any overturning process of his.

In fact, if we consider what Christ's work really consisted in, we shall perceive that it could not but be revolutionary. He was sent by God, with his Father's thoughts and this Father's will in his heart, to make those thoughts known on earth and to secure obedience to that will.

Now if the world were lovingly doing God's will to the extent of its knowledge, and anxiously seeking more knowledge in order better to obey God, then Christ's work would have been educational and not revolutionary. With words of love he would have led his willing flock to the richer pastures and purer water prepared for them. But that is not the state of the world. The crucifixion of Jesus gives the lie to that theory of life, and he that has eyes to see, can see along the track of history a long line of Calvaries, where successive generations have sought to choke the word of God calling them to righteousness. It has ever been easy for man to obey his lusts and hard to resist them. And the evil of centuries has found its proper expression and manufactured its fitting tools in the laws, the customs, the opinions and traditions prevailing in human society, so that an old man who had seen much of life, and yet loved mankind, sadly summed up his thoughts in the judgment: "The whole world is embedded in wickedness."

Now, given such a world, and given a great Christ who comes to see God's will done on earth, and in the nature of the case, there must be a collision, an upheaval, a revolutionary movement which must last and be revolutionary until either the world is brought into submission or Christ is conquered and gives up his attempt.

It is not within the purpose of this chapter to trace the course of the revolutionary movement initiated by Jesus, but simply to point out that the historical antecedents of Christianity, the contemporary forces with which it was allied, the express statements of Christ himself, the attitude of his contemporaries to him, and the very nature of his work, mite to prove that it was really a revolutionary movement. Still, a glance at the history of Christianity, as we find it in the apostolic writings of the New Testament, may serve still further to establish this point.

One of the earliest books of the New Testament in point of time is the Apocalypse. In gleaming imagery it portrays the overthrow of the brutal world powers and the inauguration of the Kingdom of Christ. In veiled words the wickedness of Rome, its luxury, its rottenness, its oppression are pictured. The Christians of that age knew what was meant by "the great city that reigns over the kings of the earth" and that "is drunk with the blood of the saints," and doubtless many hearts longed for the sounding of hallelujahs over her fall.

Another early expression of Christian thought as it prevailed among the Jewish Christians, is found in the Letter of James. There is something of the sternness of the Old Testament prophets and of John the Baptist in his rebuke of the incipient corruption of the church by property distinctions. "The faith of our Lord Jesus Christ" and the "respect of persons" seem incompatible to him. He reminds those who incline to bestow church distinctions on the man with the gold ring and the fire working, that the rich are the oppressors of the church and the blasphemers of Christ's work; while the poor are the ones whom God has chosen to be heirs of the Kingdom. Read this and see whether it sounds like complacent justification of existing conditions: "Go to now, ye rich, weep and howl for your miseries that are coming upon you. Your riches are corrupted, and your garments are moth-eaten. Your gold and your silver are rusted and their rust shall be for a testimony against you and shall eat your flesh as

fire. Ye have laid up your treasure in the last days. Behold the
hire of the laborers who mowed your fields, which is of you
kept back by fraud, crieth out; and the cries of them that reaped
have entered into the ears of the Lord of Sabaoth." [James 5,
1–4] Such thoughts were probably far more general in the early
church than we now suppose. The force and the bulk of Paul's
teaching have in our minds overshadowed everything else in the
Apostolic church.

With Paul the revolutionary element is not so dominant. His
mind worked in other directions and elaborated the thoughts
of his Master on another side. But the evil of the present state
of things, the certainty of an approaching Messianic judgment,
and the establishment of a new world era were among his
fundamental teachings. In fact he did do revolutionary work.
However much and truthfully he protested that he was establishing the law, he was really making it unnecessary; he was
leveling the distinctive prerogatives of the Jews and subvert-
ing everything in which they put their trust and pride. They
were not altogether wrong when they called him "the man that
teacheth all men everywhere against the people, and the law,
and this place," and when they repeated before Felix the charge
they had raised against Christ before Pilate: "we have found
this man a pestilent fellow and a mover of insurrections among
all the Jews throughout the world." There was truth in it. So far
as Judaism was concerned, the whole intertwined mass of its
religion, its politics and its society, Paul's work was revolutionary. And in heathen civilization he dropped a living seed which
in the course of its growth was to burst asunder the masonry
of its edifice and make it totter and fail. Very early men felt that
he was attacking the principle of unity which held the Roman
world together. It was not a mere misunderstanding when men
accused him of turning the world upside down and of oppos-
ing Caesar by proclaiming Jesus as king (Acts 17, 7). We pass
lightly over the passages in which he speaks of Christ as superior to "all government and authority and power and lordship

and every name that is named," and calls him "the blessed and only Potentate; the King of kings and Lord of lords." But in those days of abject servility to human power, when the statue of the emperor stood in every market-place and divine honor was paid to the lord of the earth, we incline to think the Christians feel those words to be more than pious phrases. At any rate the emperors soon came to feel the subversive power of these religious thoughts.

THE KINGDOM OF GOD

What, now is the aim of this revolutionary movement inaugurated by Jesus? What word is inscribed on the banner he raised?

"The Kingdom of God"! That is the phrase forever recurring in his teaching. About that his thoughts circle like a host of planets round a central sun.

And what is the "Kingdom of God"? Jesus discusses many aspects of it, its value, its laws of growth, its blessings, its obstacles; but for a definition of what he meant by the words we look in vain. Why? Because his hearers were familiar with the words and with the idea contained in them. Jesus did not create the conception. It was there; the heritage of his nation's past, and the most living hope of its present. Therefore to understand Jesus we must put ourselves in the position of his contemporaries and realize in our own mind the ideas with which the past had stocked the common mind of the Jewish people.

The conceptions which ruled the religious life of Israel were the idea of the covenant and the theocracy. Jehovah had chosen Israel as peculiarly his own. He fought its battles through the Judges. He reigned through the kings. He gave the laws. He spoke through the prophets. He heard the prayers of his people and interfered against their oppressors. If the people walked in his law, his blessing was promised to be upon them; they would till the ground in peace; the harvests would not fail; sickness would not come nigh them; their children would multiply like the young lambs of the flock. That is the Jewish ideal of life: a righteous community, ordered by divine laws, governed by God's ministers, having intercourse with the Most High, and blessed by him with the good things of life.

But the realization lagged wearily behind the ideal. The people were recreant to their obligations. The kings were more often creatures of the harem than vice-gerents of God. We hear the passionate protests of the prophets against the venality of judges and the covetousness of the nobles, and in the Psalms the poor and meek sob for redress of wrongs. The national independence was lost. The rivers of Babylon saw the mute grief of Jewish exiles. After the return Jerusalem was ground under the heels of successive oppressors.

But the faith of this wonderful nation rose triumphant above this contradiction between their faith in a sublime vocation and their actual wretchedness. Its spirit was not crushed. Its faith was not relinquished. It must have fulfilment, somewhere, sometime. The perfect reign of God in Israel would yet be. Fair above the failures of the present rose the image of a glorious future. It took its outlines from periods of prosperity in the past, and its colors were pressed from the woes of the present. Every prophet saw it darkly and prophesied in part, but every one added some touch and its lineaments grew ever clearer, till all the nation fixed its eyes on that hope.

It is not possible to trace here the long development of the Messianic hope, and the various forms it assumed in the two parts of Isaiah, in Ezekiel, in Daniel, and in the abundant apocalyptic literature after the exile. Its historic continuity was never broken, and in the days of Jesus the nation was full of eager anticipation of the Messiah's coming who was to initiate the new era by a mighty display of power in the judgment of the wicked and the liberation of the people of God.

The Messianic hope, then, was the hope for the perfection of the theocracy. Its contents varied with the character of those who entertained it. The majority perhaps looked for national revenge and temporal enjoyment. Some hoped for spiritual quickening. But this was common to them all, including John the Baptist; this belongs to the essence of the Messianic hope: that the theocratic idea was at last to have its perfect realization in a Kingdom of God on earth, with the Messiah as its head, Israel as its dwelling place and organ, and all the world as the sphere of its manifestation.

Now what attitude did Jesus assume toward the Messianic hope of his day? Did he oppose it as wrong, foolish and perilous? Was he indifferent to it, as to something remote from his own work? Or did he accept it, elevate it, and strive to realize it?

Evidently the latter. He used the vocabulary of the Messianic movement. He selected his followers from the circle most imbued with Messianic ideas. His attitude and preaching could not have been, and indeed were not, understood by his hearers as referring to anything but the fulfilment of the common hope of the nation.

The assertion that Jesus identified himself with the Messianic hope, does not imply that he proposed to fulfil every hope of every one of his contemporaries, nor even that he agreed with the conceptions entertained by a majority of them. That hope was a growth of centuries and its end was not identical with its inception. It was a popular idea that shaded off into innumerable tints, and not a rigid formula or scheme that had to be accepted entire or rejected entire. In agreeing with some Jesus could not help disagreeing with others. But the essence of the hope he must have accepted, else his words would have been misleading, and he would not have been Israel's Messiah, the fulfiller of its national religious life. If he protested that not one iota of the law should perish till it had come to its fill fruition, he could not cast aside as false or useless the central idea of the Old Testament, the idea of the theocracy, the hope of God's perfect reign in humanity.

Two things are essential to the program formulated in Christ's revolutionary parole: First, the idea of a kingdom necessarily implies a social ideal; it speaks of a perfect community. Secondly the fulfilment of that ideal is expected on this earth and on the hither side of death. "Thy Kingdom come; thy will be done on earth."

3

The Kingdom of God

This is a statement of the Brotherhood of the Kingdom that Rauschenbusch founded with fellow Baptist ministers Nathaniel Schmidt and Leighton Williams while pastors in Hell's Kitchen in New York City. It was published in the City Vigilant *in May 1894.*

An organization has recently been formed by Christian believers called "the Brotherhood of the Kingdom." Its members believe that the idea of a kingdom of God on earth was the central thought of Jesus, and ought ever to be the great aim of the church. They are convinced that this aim has largely dropped out of sight, or has been misunderstood, and that much of the social ineffectiveness of church life is due to this misunderstanding.

As we contemplated these blemishes of the body of Christ, and sorrowed over them in common with all earnest lovers of the church of Jesus, it grew clear to us that many of these evils have their root in the wrongful abandonment or the perversion of the great aim of Christ: the Kingdom of God. As the idea of the Kingdom is the key to the teachings and work of Christ, so its abandonment or misconstruction is the key to the false or one-sided conceptions of Christianity and our halting realization of it. Because the Kingdom of God has been dropped as the primary and comprehensive aim of Christianity, and personal salvation has been substituted for it, therefore men seek

40

to save their own souls and are selfishly indifferent to the evangelization of the world. Because the individualistic conception
of personal salvation has pushed out of sight the collective idea
of a Kingdom of God on earth, Christian men seek for the
salvation of individuals and are comparatively indifferent to
the spread of the spirit of Christ in the political, industrial,
social, scientific, and artistic life of humanity, and have left
these as the undisturbed possessions of the spirit of the world.
Because the Kingdom of God has been understood as a state to
be inherited in a future life rather than as something to be realized here and now, therefore Christians have been contented
with a low plane of life here and have postponed holiness to
the future. Because the Kingdom of God has been confounded
with the Church, therefore the Church has been regarded as an
end instead of a means, and men have thought they were building up the Kingdom when they were only cementing a strong
church organization.

As these thoughts took shape through observation and the
study of Scripture and church history, and grew hot through
prayer, and as we felt in our personal efforts the magnitude of
the task of removing these evils, we determined to strike hands
in the name of Christ, and by union to multiply our opportunities, increase our wisdom, and keep steadfast our courage. So
we formed ourselves into a "Brotherhood of the Kingdom," in
order "to reestablish this idea in the thought of the church and
to assist in its practical realization in the world."

We desire to see the Kingdom of God once more the great
object of Christian preaching; the inspiration of Christian hym-
nology; the foundation of systematic theology; the enduring
motive of evangelistic and missionary work; the religious inspiration of social work and the social outcome of religious inspiration; the object to which a Christian man surrenders his life,
and in that surrender saves it to eternal life; the common object
in which all religious bodies find their unity; the great synthesis
in which the regeneration of the spirit, the enlightenment of the

intellect, the development of the body, the reform of political life, the sanctification of industrial life, and all that concerns the redemption of humanity shall be embraced.

The idea of "the Kingdom of God" has gone through many changes in the history of Christianity. At present we can distinguish five different senses in which the term is used.

1. The common people generally understand by the "Kingdom of God," or the "Kingdom of Heaven," the blessed life after death—heaven. It is a condition to which they expect to go, and not a condition which they expect to come to them. Perhaps the most vivid proof for the prevalence of this conception of the "Kingdom" is the fact that the description of the New Jerusalem, in the Book of Revelation, is popularly supposed to describe heaven, while the author meant to describe the perfect city to be established on earth at the return of Christ.

2. Men of a mystical mind have usually seized on the idea of "the Kingdom of God" to designate that inner life of the Spirit which to their minds constitutes the highest gift of Christianity. Men of that turn of mind frequently slight the questions of dogma and of ecclesiastical organizations which absorb others, and they need some term not stamped with a technical sense by church usage. Their favorite passage is "The Kingdom of God is within you."

3. Men of ecclesiastical temper use the term synonymously with the "Church." The church sums up the total of divine forces in the world to their minds, and so they can make the kingdom coterminous with the church.

4. Men with whom the second coming of Christ is a living hope have restricted the term to the reign of Christ to be established after his return.

5. Men who are interested in movements that extend beyond the existing work of the church, and are pushing out under religious impulses into new fields of Christian

activity, have seized on this term as one large enough to include everything else plus the work to which they are giving themselves. So at the beginning of foreign missionary activity its pioneers loved to speak of "the enterprise for the extension of the Redeemer's Kingdom." And at present those who labor for a righteous social order under religious impulses always raise the standard of "the Kingdom of God."

Which of these ideas is right? We reply: they all err by defect. The Kingdom of God is larger than anything contained in any one of these ideas. It stands for the sum of all divine and righteous forces on earth. It embraces all pure aspirations God-ward and all due hopes for the perfection of life. It is a synthesis combining all the conceptions mentioned above, and if we could combine them in such a synthesis, it would prove to be like some chemical compounds, more powerful than the sum of all its parts.

1. In the common conceptions of the Kingdom as heaven, we must recognize the truth that we have here no abiding city. Life at its best is transitory and unsatisfactory. The perfection of our personality is not attained on earth. Even if humanity lives on and marches toward the golden city of the Ideal, the weary toiler to whom its progress is due drops by the wayside and his feet never enter the city of his longings. An ideal which is to satisfy all the desires of the human heart and is to embrace perfect man as well as the perfect Man must include a heaven beyond death.

2. In the mystical conception of the Kingdom as the inward fellowship with God, we must recognize the justice of human yearning for the living God. A righteous and happy intercourse with our fellowmen, in a true human society, will not satisfy the heart completely. Deeper than the hunger and thirst for the justice of God lies the hunger and thirst for God himself. It would be a mistake on the

part of those who labor for a perfect humanity to rule out the efforts of religion to bring men into personal intercourse with the living God.

3. We must recognize the importance of a living church within the Kingdom. It must not dwindle. It is the channel through which ethical impulses pour into humanity from God. Yet the church and the Kingdom are not identical. We are the church as we worship together; we are the Kingdom as we live justly and lovingly with one another.

4. We must recognize the justice of the millennial hopes. They stand for the force of cataclysms in human history; for the direct interference of God in the life of nations; and for the ultimate victory of right and love in the conflict of the ages.

5. But finally, we must insist that the Kingdom is not only in heaven but is to come on earth; that while it begins in the depths of the heart, it is not to stay there; that the church does not embrace all the forces of the Kingdom and is but a means for the advancement of the Kingdom; that while the perfection of the Kingdom may be reserved for a future epoch, the Kingdom is here and at work. The Kingdom means individual men and women who freely do the will of God, and who therefore live rightly with their fellowmen. And without a goodly number of such men and women, no plan for a higher social order will have stability enough to work. But the Kingdom also means a growing perfection in the collective life of humanity, in our laws, in the customs of society, in the institutions for education, and for the administration of mercy; in our public opinion, our literary and artistic ideals, in the pervasiveness of the sense of duty, and in our readiness to give our life as a ransom for others. With most social reformers, it is the former aspect which needs emphasis; with most religious people, it is the latter.

4

The New Evangelism

This selection is taken from Walter Rauschenbusch's "The New Evangelism" (1904). Rauschenbusch holds that the old *evangelism concerned itself with personal piety and salvation, and the* new *evangelism must focus on social and commercial salvation, particularly from the evils of capitalism.*

The present interest in the "New Evangelism" is almost wholly an expression of dissatisfaction with the old evangelism, the waning power of which is generally conceded. There is as yet no new evangelism before us which we might adopt; we are only wishing that there might be. Our conceptions of what it ought to be are vague, as all ideas about the future necessarily are, but that is no cause for belittling the current inquiry. It is one of the most important topics that could be discussed. I shall attempt in the following discussion to apply the same method of historical investigation to this great and threatening fact of contemporary religious history which would be applied to a fact of equal importance in a past era.

The Gospel of Christ is one and immutable; the comprehension and expression of it in history has been of infinite variety. No individual, no Church, no age of history has ever comprehended the full scope of God's saving purposes in Jesus Christ. Neither has any proclaimed it without foreign admixtures that clogged and thwarted it. A fuller and purer expression of the evangel has therefore always been possible and desirable. It is on the face of it unlikely that the Gospel as commonly understood by us is the whole Gospel or a completely pure Gospel. It is a lack of Christian humility to assume that our Gospel and the Gospel are identical.

Every individual reconstructs his comprehension of life and duty, of the world and God, as he passes from one period of development to the next. If he fails to do so, his religion will lose its grasp and control. In the same way humanity must reconstruct its moral and religious synthesis whenever it passes from one era to another. When all other departments of life and thought are silently changing it is impossible for religion to remain unaffected. The Gospel, to have power over an age, must be the highest expression of the moral and religious truths held by that age. If it lags behind and presents outgrown conceptions of life and duty, it is no longer in the full sense the Gospel. Christianity itself lifts the minds of men to demand a better expression of Christianity. If the official wardens of the Gospel from selfish motives or from conservative veneration for old statements refuse to let the Spirit of Christ flow into the larger vessels of thought and feeling which God himself has prepared for it, they are warned by finding men turn from their message as sapless and powerless. The most familiar instance is that of the Revival of Learning and the repudiation of medieval religion and theology in the fifteenth and sixteenth centuries.

We are today passing through an historical transition as thorough and important as any in history. The last 125 years have swept us through profound changes in every direction. Worldwide commerce and the imperialistic policy of the Christian nations have made the problems of international and inter-racial relations urgent. The Church responded by a new movement of world-wide missions, but it has failed hitherto to Christianize international politics. The monarchical system, so intimately connected with ancient religion, has crumbled, and democracy has taken its place; but the Church has not broadened its ethical teaching to any great extent to meet the new duties of the citizen-kings. It still confines its ethics to the personal and family life. In industry and commerce there has been a vast increase in the production of wealth and a shifting in its distribution, but the Church has furnished no adequate principles either for the distribution or the consumption of wealth. We are emerging from the era of individualism. The principle of coordination, co-operation and solidarity is being applied in ever widening areas and is gaining remarkable hold on the spirits of men. The Church is applying that principle in its organization, but its message is still chiefly on the basis of individualism.

It is not strange if the message of the Church has failed to keep pace with a movement so rapid. But neither is it strange if humanity, amid the pressure of such new problems, fails to be stirred and guided by statements of truth that were adequate to obsolete conditions. The Church is in the position of a mother talking to her son of seventeen, as if he were still twelve. What she says is good and loving, but it is not what the boy with his new passions and problems needs.

The present paralysis of the churches affects all Western Christendom and only a cause co-terminus with modern civilization will explain it. Communities are affected in just the degree in which they are affected by the progress of civilization—the backward countries and rural communities least, the industrial cities most. State churches and free churches alike feel the drag. It is not because the religious spirit has failed. It runs surprisingly strong, but it runs largely outside of the churches. Neither is the trouble due to lack of piety in the ministry, for, on the whole, we are as good as our fathers. We are told that the Gospel has always met with indifference and hostility. But is this today a persecution for righteousness' sake, so that Jesus would call us blessed for enduring it, or is it a case where the salt is trodden under foot of men, because it has lost its saltness? The worst explanation is that which shrugs its shoulders and regards

the present alienation of the people from the Church as a myste-
rious dispensation of Providence against which we are helpless.
Effects do not happen without causes, and God's reign is a reign
of law. In short, no small or local or passing cause will explain
so large a fact as the present condition of the Church.

Now, apply this to evangelism. Evangelism is only the cutting
edge of the Church, and it is driven by the weight back of it. The
evangelizing power of the Church depends on its moral prestige
and spiritual authority. Every evangelist banks on the accumu-
lated moral capital of the Church Universal.

There are two kinds of evangelization. The one proclaims new
truth, as Jesus did to his nation, or Paul to the Gentiles, or as a
missionary does to the heathen. The other summons men to live
and act according to the truth which the Church has previously
instilled into their minds and which they have long accepted as
true. The latter is, on the whole, the kind which we have to do.
To be effective, evangelism must appeal to motives which pow-
erfully seize men, and it must hold up a moral standard so high
above their actual lives that it will smite them with the conviction of sin. If the motives urged seem untrue or remote, or if
the standard of life to which they are summoned is practically
that on which they are living, the evangelistic call will have little
power. The two questions which every Christian worker should
investigate for himself are these: Are the traditional motives still
effective? And is the moral standard held up by the Church such
as to induce repentance?

The motives urged at any time will vary with the preacher and
the audience, and there will always be a large measure of truth
and power even in the most defective preaching that touches
human nature at all. Yet there is a change in emphasis from age
to age. Within our own memory the fear of hell and the desire
for bliss in heaven have strangely weakened, even with men who
have no doubt of the reality of hell and heaven. On the other
hand, the insistence on present holiness and Christian living
has strengthened. Good men give less thought to their personal

salvation than our fathers, but their sympathy for the sorrows of others is more poignant. Past Christianity has developed in us a love for our fellows and a sense of solidarity so strong that they demand to be considered in every religious appeal. On the other hand, we cannot conceal from ourselves that the old "scheme of salvation" seems mechanical and remote, and its effectiveness as a motive depends largely on the past teaching of it, which is stored in our minds. The sense of great coming changes, begotten by a better knowledge of the plastic possibilities of mankind, is strong upon us. We have a new hope for humanity such as has long existed only where the millennial hope was a vital thing.

Even so brief an enumeration must make us feel that some motives are dropping away, because they were narrow and incompletely Christian, and larger and more truly Christ-like motives are offering themselves. It should be the scientific effort of every Christian worker to observe what motives are to-day really effective with the young and thoughtful minds who represent the present and the future. The fact that some evangelists who are determined in repudiating anything that savors of "modern thought" are so effective in urging the old motives does not invalidate what we have said. In every large city there are many men who belong to the old time and are untouched as yet by the new. They respond joyfully to the ideas in which their Christian life was nurtured and in which their holiest memories are enshrined. But there are other men who come once and then stay away, because they hear nothing to which they can respond. And these men are not counted. Moreover, the strong personality of the evangelist may count for more than anything he says.

What about the moral standard held up by the Church in its teaching and in its collective life? Can she summon men to repentance by it?

The moral teaching of the Church in the past has dealt with private and family life. It has boldly condemned drunkenness, sexual impurity, profanity; it has fostered gentleness and pity; and it has been largely successful in this teaching. It has also drawn the line against Sabbath breaking, dancing, card-playing and theater-going, but it has not been successful in maintaining that line. In general, the community has risen toward the level of the Church in private and domestic virtue, and the Church has drifted toward the level of the respectable community in regard to amusements. As a result of both movements the gap has lessened. The morality of the Church is not much more than what prudence, respectability and good breeding also demand. Nor is the morality of church members generally distinguished by the glow of spiritual fervor. There is less family worship and prayerful life than with our fathers. But with this moral outfit can the Church authoritatively say to the world, "Repent and become like me?"

When we pass from private and domestic life to political and business life the matter is worse. About the most pressing questions arising there the Church as a body is dumb. It has nothing to say about the justice of holding land idle in crowded cities, of appropriating the unearned increment in land values, of paying wages fixed by the hunger of the laborers and taking the surplus of their output as "profits," or of cornering the market in the necessaries of life. It feels restless about some glaring evils like child-labor, but only moderately so. Individuals in the Church are intelligent and active, but the Church, both as an organized body and as a corporate spiritual force, is inert. The moral guide of humanity is silent where authoritative speech is today most needed. Where it does speak, it is often on the wrong side. When we consider the ideas prevalent in the churches, their personnel, and their sources of income, has the Church a message of repentance and an evangel for this modern world?

One important and growing class in our population is largely alienated from the Church—namely, the industrial wage-workers. The alienation is most complete where the development under the capitalistic system has most completely run its course. In our country that alienation has begun within the last generation, during which this class has become a class, and the process is not yet complete. This constitutes the spiritual barrier to evangelistic efforts as soon as they go beyond the young people of the families already in the churches. Our evangelistic call strikes an invisible wall and comes back in hollow echoes. It is an untrue and cruel charge to say that the Church workers have not done their best to reach the people. The efforts of the churches in the great cities for the last generation have perhaps never been paralleled. And yet they are futile. This is one of the most stunning and heart-rending facts in all our life.

The Church has passed under the spiritual domination of the commercial and professional classes. I do not mean that they alone compose its membership; but they furnish its chief support, do its work, and their ethics and views of life determine the thought of the Church more than we realize. This is not due to any wrongful attempt to make the Church subservient, but rather to the fact that they are the dominant classes in all industrial nations, in literature and politics, as well as in the Church. Now the stratification of society is becoming more definite in our country, and the people are growing more conscious of it. The industrial conflicts make them realize how their interests diverge from those of the commercial class. As that consciousness increases, it becomes harder for the two classes to meet in the expression of Christian faith and love—in prayer meetings, for instance. When the Christian business man is presented as a model Christian, working people are coming to look with suspicion on these samples of our Christianity. I am not justifying that, but simply stating the fact. They disapprove of the Christianity of the churches, not because it is too good, but because it is not good enough. The working people are now developing the principle and practice of solidarity, which promises to be one of the most potent ethical forces of the future, and which is essentially more Christian than the covetousness and selfishness which we regard as the indispensable basis of commerce. If this is a correct diagnosis of our condition, is it strange that the Church is unable to evangelize a class alienated from it by divergent class interest and class morality?

Let us sum up. The powerlessness of the old evangelism is only the most striking and painful demonstration of the general state of the churches. Its cause is not local nor temporary. It does not lie in lack of hard work or of prayer or of keen anxiety. It lies in the fact that modern life has gone through immense changes and the Church has not kept pace with it in developing the latent moral and spiritual resources of the Gospel which are needed by the new life. It has most slighted that part of the Gospel which our times most need. It lacks an ethical imperative which can induce repentance. In private life its standard differs little from respectability. In commerce and industry, where the unsolved and painful problems lie, it has no clear message, and often claims to be under no obligation to have one. In the State Churches the State has dominated; in the free Churches the capitalist class dominates. Both influences are worldly—in favor of things as they are and against the ideals which animate the common people. The people are becoming daily more sensitive to the class cleavage of society. The church suffers under the general resentment against the class with which it is largely identified. To this must be added the fact that the spirit of free inquiry engendered by modern science neutralizes the dogmatic authority with which the Church has been accustomed to speak.

The new evangelism which shall overcome these barriers and again exert the full power of the Gospel cannot be made to order nor devised by a single man. It will be the slow product of the fearless thought of many honest men. It will have to retain all that was true and good in the old synthesis, but advance the human conception of salvation one stage closer to the divine conception. It will have to present a conception of God, of life, of duty, of destiny, to which the best religious life of our age will bow. It will have to give an adequate definition of how a Christian man should live under modern conditions, and then summon men to live so.

A compelling evangel for the working class will be wrought out only by men who love that class, share its life, understand the ideals for which it is groping, penetrate those ideals with the religious spirit of Christianity, and then proclaim a message in which the working people will find their highest self. They will never be reached by a middle class gospel preached down at them with the consciousness of superiority.

If we personally are to have a share in working out the new evangel, we shall have to be open to two influences and allow them to form a vital union in our personalities. We must open our minds to the spirit of Jesus in its primitive, uncorrupted and still unexhausted power. That spirit is the fountain of youth for the church. As a human organization it grows old and decrepit like every other human organism. But again and again it has been rejuvenated by a new baptism in that Spirit. We must also keep our vision dear to the life of our own time. Our age is as sublime as any in the past. It has a right to its own appropriation and understanding of the Gospel. By the decay of the old, God himself is forcing us on to seek the new and higher.

This attempt at a diagnosis of our ills is not offered in a spirit of condemnation, but of personal repentance and heart-searching. We all bear our share of guilt. I have full faith in the future of the Christian church. A new season of power will come when we have put our sin from us. Our bitter need will drive us to repentance. The prophetic Spirit will awaken among us. The tongue of fire will descend on twentieth century men and give them great faith, joy and boldness, and then we shall hear the new evangel, and it will be the Old Gospel.

5

What to Do

This is perhaps the most challenging chapter of Rauschenbusch's most notable work, Christianity and the Social Crisis *(1907). He describes the evils of capitalist society and examines socialism and other reform movements as a solution to the suffering of the poor and disenfranchised.*

The ideal of a fraternal organization of society is so splendid that it is to-day enlisting the choicest young minds of the intellectual classes under its banner. Idealists everywhere are surrendering to it, especially those who are under the power of the ethical spirit of Christianity. The influence which these idealists exert in reinforcing the movement toward solidarity is beyond computation. They impregnate the popular mind with faith and enthusiasm. They furnish the watch-words and the intellectual backing of historical and scientific information. They supply devoted leaders and give a lofty sanction to the movement by their presence in it. They diminish the resistance of the upper classes among whom they spread their ideas.

But we must not blink at the fact that the idealists alone have never carried through any great social change. In vain they dash their fair ideas against the solid granite of human selfishness. The possessing classes are strong by mere possession long-continued. They control nearly all property. The law is on their side, for they have made it. They control the machinery of government and can use force under the form of law. Their self-interest makes them almost impervious to moral truth if it calls in question the sources from which they draw their income. In the past they have laughed at the idealists if they seemed harmless, or have suppressed them if they became troublesome.

We Americans have a splendid moral optimism. We believe that "truth is mighty and must prevail." "Truth crushed to earth shall rise again." "The blood of the martyrs is the seed of the Church." In the words of the great Anabaptist Balthaser Hübmaier, who attested his faith by martyrdom, "Truth is immortal; and though for a long time she be imprisoned, scourged, crowned with thorns, crucified and buried, she will yet rise victorious on the third day and will reign and triumph." That is a glorious faith. But the three days may be three centuries, and the murdered truth may never rise again in the nation that crucified it, but may come to victory in some other race and on another continent. The Peasants' Rising in 1525 in Germany embodied the social ideals of the common people; the Anabaptist movement, which began simultaneously, expressed their religious aspirations; both were essentially noble and just; both have been most amply justified by the later course of history; yet both were quenched in streams of blood and have had to wait till our own day for their resurrection in new form.

Truth is mighty. But for a definite historical victory a given truth must depend on the class which makes that truth its own and fights for it. If that class is sufficiently numerous, compact, intelligent, organized, and conscious of what it wants, it may drive a breach through the entrenchments of those opposed to it and carry the cause to victory. If there is no such army to fight its cause, the truth will drive individuals to a comparatively fruitless martyrdom and will continue to hover over humanity as a disembodied ideal. There were a number of reformatory movements before 1500 which looked fully as promising and powerful as did the movement led by Luther in its early years;

but the fortified authority of the papacy and clergy succeeded in frustrating them, and they ebbed away again. The Lutheran and Calvinistic Reformation succeeded because they enlisted classes which were sufficiently strong politically and economically to defend the cause of Reformed religion. It was only when concrete material interests entered into a working alliance with Truth that enough force was rallied to break down the frowning walls of error. On the other hand, the classes within which Anabaptism gained lodgment lacked that concrete power, and so the Anabaptist movement, which promised for a short time to be the real Reformation of Germany, just as it came to be the real Reformation of England in the Commonwealth, died a useless and despised death. In the French Revolution the ideal of democracy won a great victory, not simply because the ideal was so fair, but because it represented the concrete interests of the strong, wealthy, and intelligent business class, and that class was able to wrest political control from the king, the aristocracy, and the clergy.

The question is whether the ideal of cooperation and economic fraternity can to-day depend on any great and conquering class whose self-interest is bound up with the victory of that principle. It is hopeless to expect the business class to espouse that principle as a class. Individuals in the business class will do so, but the class will not. There is no historical precedent for an altruistic self-effacement of a whole class. Of the professional class it is safe to expect that an important minority—perhaps a larger minority in our country than in any county heretofore—will range themselves under the new social ideal. With them especially the factor of religion will prove of immense power. But their motives will in the main be idealistic, and in the present stage of man's moral development the unselfish emotions are fragile and easily chafe through, unless the coarse fiber of self-interest is woven into them. But there is another class to which that conception of organized fraternity is not only a moral ideal, but the hope for bread and butter; with which it enlists not only religious devotion and self-sacrifice, but involves salvation from poverty and insecurity and participation in the wealth and culture of modern life for themselves and their children.

It is a mistake to regard the French Revolution as a movement of the poor. The poor fought in the uprising, but the movement got its strength, its purpose, and its direction from the "third estate," the bourgeoisie, the business class of the cities, and they alone drew lasting profit from it. That class had been slowly rising to wealth, education, and power for several centuries, and the democratic movement of the nineteenth century has in the main been their march to complete ascendency.

During the same period we can watch the slow development of a new class, which has been called the fourth estate: the city working class, the wage-workers. They form a distinct class, all living without capital merely by the sale of their labor, working and living under similar physical and social conditions everywhere, with the same economic interests and the same points of view. They present a fairly homogeneous body and if any section of the people forms a "class," they do. The massing of labor in the factories since the introduction of power machinery has brought them into close contact with one another. Hard experience has taught them how helpless they are when they stand alone. They have begun to realize their solidarity and the divergence of their interests from those of the employers. They have begun to organize and are slowly learning to act together. The spread of education and cheap literature, the ease of communication, and the freedom of public meeting have rapidly created a common body of ideas and points of view among them.

The modern "labor movement" is the upward movement of this class. It began with local and concrete issues that pressed upon a given body of workingmen some demand for shorter hours or better wages, some grievance about fines or docking. The trades-unions were formed as defensive organizations for collective action. It is quite true that they have often been foolish and tyrannical in their demands, and headstrong and even lawless in their actions; but if we consider the insecurity and narrowness of the economic existence of the working people, and the glaring contrast between the meagre reward for their labor and the dazzling returns given to invested capital, it is impossible to deny that they have good cause for making a strenuous and continuous fight for better conditions of life. If Christian men are really interested in the salvation of human lives and in the health, the decency, the education, and the morality of the people, they must wish well to the working people in their effort to secure such conditions for themselves and their dear ones that they will not have to die of tuberculosis in their prime, nor feel their strength ground down by long hours of work, nor see their women and children drawn into the merciless hopper of factory labor, nor be shut out from the enjoyment of the culture about them which they have watered with their sweat.

But the labor movement means more than better wages and shorter hours for individual workingmen. It involves the struggle for a different status for their entire class. Other classes have long ago won a recognized standing in law and custom and public opinion—so long ago that they have forgotten that they ever had to win it. For instance, the medical profession is recognized by law; certain qualifications are fixed for admission to it; certain privileges are granted to those inside; irregular practitioners are hampered or suppressed. The clerical profession enjoys certain exemptions from taxation, military service, and jury duty; ministers have the right to solemnize marriages and collect fees therefore; railways give them half fares, and these privileges are granted to those whom the clergy themselves ordain and admit to their "closed shop." A lawyer who is admitted to the bar thereby becomes a court officer; the bar association, which is his trades-union, takes the initiative in disbarring men who violate the class code, and the courts take cognizance of its action; in the state of New York the bar associations have assumed some right to nominate the judges. As for the business class, it is so

completely enthroned in our social organization that it often
assumes that it is itself the whole of society.

On the other hand, the working class has no adequate standing as yet. It did have in the guilds of former times, but modern industry and modern law under the laissez-faire principle
dissolved the old privileges and reduced the working class to
a mass of unrelated human atoms. Common action on their
part was treated in law as conspiracy. In our country they have
not yet won from their employers nor from public opinion the
acknowledged right to be organized, to bargain collectively, and
to assist in controlling the discipline of the shops in which they
have to work. The law seems to afford them very little backing as yet. It provides penalties for the kind of injuries which
workingmen are likely to inflict on their employers, but not for
the subtler injuries which employers are likely to inflict on their
workingmen. Few will care to assert that in the bitter conflicts
waged between labor and capital the wrong has always been
on one side. Yet when the law bares its sword, it is somehow
always against one side. The militia does not seem to be ordered
out against capital. The labor movement must go on until public opinion and the law have conceded a recognized position to
the labor-unions, and until the workingmen interested in a given
question stand collectively on a footing of equality with the capitalists interested in it. This means a curtailment of power for the
employers, and it would be contrary to human nature for them
to like it. But for the working class it would be suicidal to forego
the attempt to get it. They have suffered fearfully by not having
it. All the sacrifices they may bring in the chronic industrial war-
fare of the present will be cheap if they ultimately win through
to an assured social and legal status for their class.

As long as the working class simply attempts to better its condition somewhat and to secure a recognized standing for its class
organization, it stands on the basis of the present capitalistic
organization of industry. Capitalism necessarily divides industrial society into two classes, those who own the instruments

and materials of production, and those who furnish the labor for it. This sharp division is the peculiar characteristic of modern capitalism which distinguishes it from other forms of social organization in the past. These two classes have to cooperate in modern production. The labor movement seeks to win better terms for the working class in striking its bargains. Yet whatever terms organized labor succeeds in winning are always temporary and insecure, like the hold which a wrestler gets on the body of his antagonist. The persistent tendency with capital necessarily is to get labor as cheaply as possible and to force as much work from it as possible. Moreover, labor is always in an inferior position in the struggle. It is handicapped by its own hunger and lack of resources. It has to wrestle on its knees with a foreman who is on his feet. Is this unequal struggle between two conflicting interests to go on forever? Is this insecurity the best that the working class can ever hope to attain?

Here enters socialism. It proposes to abolish the division of industrial society into two classes and to close the fatal chasm which has separated the employing class from the working class since the introduction of power machinery. It proposes to restore the independence of the workingman by making him once more the owner of his tools and to give him the full proceeds of his production instead of a wage determined by his poverty. It has no idea of reverting to the simple methods of the old handicrafts, but heartily accepts the power machinery, the great factory, the division of labor, the organization of the men in great regiments of workers, as established facts in modern life, and as the most efficient method of producing wealth. But it proposes to give to the whole body of workers the ownership of these vast instruments of production and to distribute among them all the entire proceeds of their common labor. There would then be no capitalistic class opposed to the working class; there would be a single class which would unite the qualities of both. Every workman would be both owner and worker, just as a farmer is who tills his own farm, or a housewife who works in her own kitchen. This

would be a permanent solution of the labor question. It would
end the present insecurity, the constant antagonism, the social
inferiority, the physical exploitation, the intellectual poverty to
which the working class is now exposed even when its condition
is most favorable.

If such a solution is even approximately feasible, it should be
hailed with joy by every patriot and Christian, for it would put
a stop to our industrial war, drain off the miasmatic swamp of
undeserved poverty, save our political democracy, and lift the
great working class to an altogether different footing of comfort,
intelligence, security and moral strength. And it would embody
the principle of solidarity and fraternity in the fundamental institutions of our industrial life. All the elements of cooperation and
interaction which are now at work in our great establishments
would be conserved, and in addition the hearty interest of all
workers in their common factory or store would be immensely
intensified by the diffused sense of ownership. Such a social
order would develop the altruistic and social instincts just as the
competitive order brings out the selfish instincts.

Socialism is the ultimate and logical outcome of the labor
movement. When the entire working class throughout the
industrial nations is viewed in large way, the progress of socialism gives an impression of resistless and elemental power. It is
inconceivable from the point of view of that class that it should
stop short of complete independence and equality as long as it
has the power to move on, and independence and equality for
the working class must mean the collective ownership of the
means of production and the abolition of the present two-class
arrangement of industrial society. If the labor movement in our
country is only slightly tinged with socialism as yet, it is merely
because it is still in its embryonic stages. Nothing will bring the
working class to a thorough comprehension of the actual status
of their class and its ultimate aim more quickly than continued
failure to secure their smaller demands and reactionary efforts
to suppress their unions.

We started out with the proposition that the ideal of a fraternal organization of society will remain powerless if it is supported by idealists only; that it needs the firm support of a solid class whose economic future is staked on the success of that ideal; and that the industrial working class is consciously or unconsciously committed to the struggle for the realization of that principle. It follows that those who desire the victory of that ideal from a religious point of view will have to enter into a working alliance with this class. Just as the Protestant principle of religious liberty and the democratic principle of political liberty rose to victory by an alliance with the middle class which was then rising to power, so the new Christian principle of brotherly association must ally itself with the working class if both are to conquer. Each depends on the other. The idealistic movement alone would be a soul without a body; the economic class movement alone would be a body without a soul. It needs the high elation and faith that come through religion. Nothing else will call forth that self-sacrificing devotion and lifelong fidelity which will be needed in so gigantic a struggle as lies before the working class.

The cooperation of professional men outside the working class would contribute scientific information and trained intelligence. They would mediate between the two classes, interpreting each to the other, and thereby lessening the strain of hostility. Their presence and sympathy would cheer the working people and diminish the sense of class isolation. By their contact with the possessing classes they could help to persuade them of the inherent justice of the labor movement and so create a leaning toward concessions. No other influence could do so much to prevent a revolutionary explosion of pent-up forces. It is to the interest of all sides that the readjustment of the social classes should come as a steady evolutionary process rather than as a social catastrophe. If the laboring class should attempt to seize political power suddenly, the attempt might be beaten back with terrible loss in efficiency to the movement. If the attempt should be successful, a raw governing class would be compelled to handle a situation so vast and complicated that no past revolution presents a parallel. There would be widespread disorder and acute distress, and a reactionary relapse to old conditions would, by all historical precedents, be almost certain to occur. It is devoutly to be desired that the shifting of power should come through a continuous series of practicable demands on one side and concessions on the other. Such an historical process will be immensely facilitated if there are a large number of men in the professional and business class with whom religious and ethical motives overcome their selfish interests so that they will throw their influence on the side of the class which is now claiming its full rights in the family circle of humanity.

On the other hand, the Christian idealists must not make the mistake of trying to hold the working class down to the use of moral suasion only, or be repelled when they hear the brute note of selfishness and anger. The class struggle is bound to be transferred to the field of politics in our country in some form. It would be folly if the working class failed to use the leverage which their political power gives them. The business class has certainly never failed to use political means to further its interests. This is a war of conflicting interests which is not likely to be fought out in love and tenderness. The possessing class will make concessions not in brotherly love but in fear, because it has to. The working class will force its demands, not merely because they are just, but because it feels it cannot do without them, and because it is strong enough to coerce. Even Bismarck acknowledged that the former indifference of the business class in Germany to the sufferings of the lower classes had not been overcome by philanthropy, but by fear of the growing discontent of the people and the spread of social democracy. Max Nordau meant the same when he said, "In spite of its theoretical absurdity, socialism has already in thirty years wrought greater amelioration than all the wisdom of statesmen and philosophers of thousands of years." All that we as Christian men can do is to ease the struggle and hasten the victory of the right by giving faith and hope to those who are down, and quickening the sense of justice with those who are in power, so that they will not harden their hearts and hold Israel in bondage, but will "let the people go." But that spiritual contribution, intangible and imponderable though it be, has a chemical power of immeasurable efficiency.

We undertook in this chapter to suggest in what ways the moral forces latent in Christian society could be mobilized for the progressive regeneration of social life, and in what directions chiefly these forces should be exerted.

We saw that some lines of effort frequently attempted in the past by Christian men and organizations are useless and misleading. It is fruitless to attempt to turn modern society back to conditions prevailing before power machinery and trusts had revolutionized it; or to copy biblical institutions adapted to wholly different social conditions; or to postpone the Christianizing of society to the millennium; or to found Christian communistic colonies within the competitive world; or to make the organized church the center and manager of an improved social machinery. The force of religion can best be applied to social renewal by sending its spiritual power along the existing and natural relations of men to direct them to truer ends and govern them by higher motives.

The fundamental contribution of every man is the change of his own personality. We must repent of the sins of existing society, cast off the spell of the lies protecting our social wrongs, have faith in a higher social order, and realize in ourselves a new type of Christian manhood which seeks to overcome the evil in the present world, not by withdrawing from the world, but by revolutionizing it.

If this new type of religious character multiplies among the young men and women, they will change the world when they come to hold the controlling positions of society in their maturer years. They will give a new force to righteous and enlightened public opinion, and will apply the religious sense of duty and service to the common daily life with a new motive and directness.

The ministry in particular, must apply the teaching functions of the pulpit to the pressing questions of public morality. It must collectively learn not to speak without adequate information; not to charge individuals with guilt in which all society shares; not to be partial, and yet to be on the side of the lost; not to yield to political partisanship, but to deal with moral questions before they become political issues and with those questions of public welfare which never do become political issues. They must lift the social questions to a religious level by faith and spiritual insight. The larger the number of ministers who attempt these untrodden ways, the safer and saner will those be who follow. By interpreting one social class to the other, they can create a disposition to make concessions and help in securing a peaceful settlement of social issues.

The force of the religious spirit should be bent toward asserting the supremacy of life over property. Property exists to maintain and develop life. It is unchristian to regard human life as a mere instrument for the production of wealth.

The religious sentiment can protect good customs and institutions against the inroads of ruthless greed, and extend their scope. It can create humane customs which the law is impotent to create. It can create the convictions and customs which are later embodied in good legislation.

Our complex society rests largely on the stewardship of delegated powers. The opportunities to profit by the betrayal of trust increase with the wealth and complexity of civilization. The most fundamental evils in past history and present conditions were due to converting stewardship into ownership. The keener moral insight created by Christianity should lend its help in scrutinizing all claims to property and power in order to detect latent public rights and to recall the recreant stewards to their duty.

Primitive society was communistic. The most valuable institutions in modern life—the family, the school and church—are
communistic. The state, too, is essentially communistic and is
becoming increasingly so. During the larger part of its history
the Christian church regarded communism as the only ideal
life. Christianity certainly has more affinity for cooperative and
fraternal institutions than for competitive disunion. It should
therefore strengthen the existing communistic institutions and
aid the evolution of society from the present temporary stage of
individualism to a higher form of communism.

The splendid ideal of a fraternal organization of society cannot be realized by idealists only. It must be supported by the
self-interest of a powerful class. The working class, which is now
engaged in its upward movement, is struggling to secure better
conditions of life, an assured status for its class organizations,
and ultimately the ownership of the means of production. Its
success in the last great aim would mean the closing of the gap
which now divides industrial society and the establishment of
industry on the principle of solidarity and the method of cooperation. Christianity should enter into a working alliance with
this rising class, and by its mediation secure the victory of these
principles by a gradual equalization of social opportunity and
power.

The first apostolate of Christianity was born from a deep fel-
low-feeling for social misery and from the consciousness of a
great historical opportunity. Jesus saw the peasantry of Gali-
lee following him about with their poverty and their diseases,
like shepherdess sheep that have been scattered and harried by
beasts of prey, and his heart had compassion on them. He felt
that the harvest was ripe, but there were few to reap it. Past
history had come to its culmination, but there were few who
understood the situation and were prepared to cope with it. He
bade his disciples to pray for laborers for the harvest, and then
made them answer their own prayers by sending them out two

by two to proclaim the kingdom of God. That was the beginning of the world-wide mission of Christianity.

The situation is repeated on a vaster scale to-day. If Jesus stood to-day amid our modern life, with that outlook on the condition of all humanity which observation and travel and the press would spread before him, and with the same heart of divine humanity beating in him, he would create a new apostolate to meet the new needs in a new harvest-time of history.

To anyone who knows the sluggishness of humanity to good, the impregnable entrenchments of vested wrongs and the long reaches of time needed from one milestone of progress to the next, the task of setting up a Christian social order in this modern world of ours seems like a fair and futile dream. Yet in fact it is not one tithe as hopeless as when Jesus set out to do it. When he told his disciples, "Ye are the salt of the earth; ye are the light of the world," he expressed the consciousness of a great historic mission to the whole of humanity. Yet it was a Nazarene carpenter speaking to a group of Galilean peasants and fishermen. Under the circumstances at that time it was an utterance of the most daring faith, faith in himself, faith in them, faith in what he was putting into them, faith in faith. Jesus failed and was crucified, first his body by his enemies, and then his spirit by his friends; but that failure was so amazing a success that to-day it takes an effort on our part to realize that it required any faith on his part to inaugurate the kingdom of God and to send out his apostolate.

To-day, as Jesus looks out upon humanity, his spirit must leap to see the souls responsive to his call. They are sown broadcast through humanity, legions of them. The harvest-field is no longer deserted. All about us we hear the clang of the whetstone and the rush of the blades through the grain and the shout of the reapers. With all our faults and our slothfulness we modern men in many ways are more on a level with the real mind of Jesus than any generation that has gone before. If that first apostolate was able to move mountains by the power of faith, such an apostolate as Christ could now summon might change the face of the earth. The apostolate of a new age must do the work of the sower. When the sower goes forth to sow his seed, he goes with the certainty of partial failure and the knowledge that a long time of patience and of hazard will intervene before he can hope to see the result of his work and his venture. In sowing the truth a man may never see or trace the results. The more ideal his conceptions are, and the farther they move ahead of his time, the larger will be the percentage of apparent failure. But he can afford to wait. The powers of life are on his side. He is like a man who has scattered his seed and then goes off to sleep by night and work by day, and all the while the seed, by the inscrutable chemistry of life, lays hold of the ingredients of its environment and builds them up to its own growth. The mustard-seed becomes a tree. The leaven assimilates the meal by biological processes. The new life penetrates the old humanity and transforms it. Robert Owen was a sower. His cooperative communities failed. He was able to help only a small fraction of the workingmen of his day. But his moral enthusiasm and his ideas fertilized the finest and most self-sacrificing minds among the working classes. They cherished his ultimate hopes in private and worked for realizable ends in public. The Chartist movement was filled with his spirit. The most influential leaders of English unionism in its great period after the middle of the nineteenth century were Owenites. The Rochdale Pioneers were under his influence, and the great cooperative movement in England, an economic force of the first importance, grew in some measure out of the seed which Owen had scattered. Other men may own the present. The future belongs to the sower—provided he scatters seed and does not mistake the chaff for it which once was so essential to the seed and now is dead and useless.

It is inevitable that those who stand against conditions in which most men believe and by which the strongest profit, shall suffer for their stand. The little group of early Christian socialists in England, led by Maurice, Kingsley, and Hughes, now stand by common consent in the history of that generation as one of its finest products, but at that time they were bitterly assailed and misunderstood. Pastor Rudolf Todt, the first man in Germany who undertook to prove that the New Testament and the ethics of socialism have a close affinity, was almost unanimously attacked by the church of Germany. But Jesus told his apostles at the outset that opposition would be part of their day's work. Christ equipped his church with no legal rights to protect her, the only political right he gave his disciples was the right of being persecuted. It is part of the doctrine of vicarious atonement, which is fundamental in Christianity, that the prophetic souls must vindicate by their sufferings the truth of the truth they preach.

> Disappointment's dry and bitter root,
> Envy's harsh berries, and the choking pool
> Of the world's scorn, are the right mother-milk
> To the tough hearts that pioneer their kind
> And break a pathway to those unknown realms
> That in the earth's broad shadow lie enthralled;
> Endurance is the crowning quality,
> And patience all the passion of great hearts;
> These are their stay, and when the leaden world
> Sets its hard face against their fateful thought,
> And brute strength, like a scornful conqueror,
> Clangs his huge mace down in the other scale,
> The inspired soul but flings his patience in,
> And slowly that outweighs the ponderous globe,
> One faith against a whole earth's unbelief,
> One soul against the flesh of all mankind.

The championship of social justice is almost the only way left open to a Christian nowadays to gain the crown of martyrdom. Theological heretics are rarely persecuted now. The only rival of

God is mammon, and it is only when his sacred name is blasphemed that men throw the Christians to the lions.

Even for the social heretics there is a generous readiness to listen which was unknown in the past. In our country that openness of mind is a product of our free intellectual life, our ingrained democracy, the denominational manifoldness of our religious life, and the spread of the Christian spirit. It has become an accepted doctrine among us that all great movements have obscure beginnings, and that belief tends to make men respectful toward anything that comes from some despised Nazareth. Unless a man forfeits respect by bitterness or lack of tact, he is accorded a large degree of tolerance, though he will always be made to feel the difference between himself and those who say the things that please the great.

The certainty of opposition constitutes a special call to the strong. The ministry seems to have little attraction for the sons of rich men. It is not strange when one considers the enervating trials that beset a rich man in a pastorate. But here is a mission that ought to appeal to the rich young man if he has heroic stuff in him. His assured social standing would give him an influence with rich and poor alike which others attain but slowly if at all. The fear of being blacklisted for championing justice and mercy need have no terrors for him. To use his property as a coat of mail in fighting the battles of the weak would be the best way of obeying Christ's command to the rich young ruler to sell all and give it to the poor. When Mr. Roosevelt was still Police Commissioner in New York, he said to the young men of New York: "I would teach the young men that he who has not wealth owes his first duty to his family, but he who has means owes his to the State. It is ignoble to go on heaping up money. I would preach the doctrine of work to all, and to the men of wealth the doctrine of unremunerative work." The most "unremunerative work" is the work that draws opposition and animosity.

Mr. Roosevelt implies here that a man's duty to his family is the first and dominant duty, and that this exempts him in some measure from service to the larger public. It follows that the childless have a call to the dangerous work of the kingdom of God. A man and woman who are feeding and training young citizens are performing so immense and absorbing a service to the future that they might well be exempt from taxes to the state and from sacrificial service to the kingdom of God. If nevertheless so many of them assume these duties in addition, the childless man and woman will have to do heroic work in the trenches before they can rank on the same level. It is not fair to ask a man with children to give his time and strength as freely to public causes as if he had none. It is still more unfair to expect him to risk the bread and the prospects of his family in championing dangerous causes as freely as if he risked only himself. The childless people should adopt the whole coming generation of children and fight to make the world more habitable for them as for their own brood. The unmarried and the childless should enlist in the new apostolate and march on the forlorn hopes with Jesus Christ.

In asking for faith in the possibility of a new social order, we ask for no Utopian delusion. We know well that there is no perfection for man in this life: there is only growth toward perfection. In personal religion we look with seasoned suspicion at any one who claims to be holy and perfect, yet we always tell men to become holy and to seek perfection. We make it a duty to seek what is unattainable. We have the same paradox in the perfectibility of society. We shall never have a perfect social life, yet we must seek it with faith. We shall never abolish suffering. There will always be death and the empty chair and heart. There will always be the agony of love unreturned. Women will long for children and never press baby lips to their breast. Men will long for fame and miss it. Imperfect moral insight will work hurt in the best conceivable social order. The strong will always have the impulse to exert their strength, and no system can be devised which can keep them from crowding and jostling the weaker. Increased social refinement will bring increased sensitiveness to pain. An American may suffer as much distress through a social slight as a Russian peasant under the knout. At best there is always but an approximation to a perfect social order. The kingdom of God is always but coming.

But every approximation to it is worthwhile. Every step toward personal purity and peace, though it only makes the consciousness of imperfection more poignant, carries its own exceeding great reward, and everlasting pilgrimage toward the kingdom of God is better than contented stability in the tents of wickedness.

And sometimes the hot hope surges up that perhaps the long and slow climb may be ending. In the past the steps of our race toward progress have been short and feeble, and succeeded by long intervals of sloth and apathy. But is that necessarily to remain the rate of advance? In the intellectual life there has been an unprecedented leap forward during the last hundred years. Individually we are not more gifted than our grandfathers, but collectively we have wrought out more epoch-making discoveries and inventions in one century than the whole race in the untold centuries that have gone before. If the twentieth century could do for us in the control of social forces what the nineteenth did for us in the control of natural forces, our grandchildren would live in a society that would be justified in regarding our present social life as semi-barbarous. Since the Reformation began to free the mind and to direct the force of religion toward morality, there has been a perceptible increase of speed. Humanity is gaining in elasticity and capacity for change, and every gain in general intelligence, in organizing capacity, in physical and moral soundness, and especially in responsiveness to ideal motives, again increases the ability to advance without disastrous reactions. The swiftness of evolution in our own country proves the immense latent perfectibility in human nature.

Last May a miracle happened. At the beginning of the week the fruit trees bore brown and greenish buds. At the end of the week they were robed in bridal garments of blossoms. But for weeks and months the sap had been rising and distending the cells and maturing the tissues which were half ready in the fall before. The swift unfolding was the culmination of a long process. Perhaps these nineteen centuries of Christian influence have been a long preliminary stage of growth, and now the flower and fruit are almost here. If at this juncture we can rally sufficient religious faith and moral strength to snap the bonds of evil and turn the present unparalleled economic and intellectual resources of humanity to the harmonious development of a true social life, the generations yet unborn will mark this as that great day of the Lord for which the ages waited, and count us blessed for sharing in the apostolate that proclaimed it.

6

Prayers

This essay and the prayers that follow are from Rauschenbusch's 1910 book, For God and the People: Prayers of the Social Awakening. *While some of the prayers reflect the tenor and mores of his day, they were considered quite radical at that time, since they championed the rights of children, women, and workers who were treated miserably by their employers. They clearly reflect Rauschenbusch's conviction that the Reign of God was at the heart of the Social Gospel.*

THE SOCIAL MEANING OF THE LORD'S PRAYER

The Lord's Prayer is recognized as the purest expression of the mind of Jesus. It crystallizes his thoughts. It conveys the atmosphere of his childlike trust in the Father. It gives proof of the transparent clearness and peace of his soul.

It first took shape as a protest against the wordy flattery with which men tried to wheedle their gods. He demanded simplicity and sincerity in all expressions of religion, and offered this as an example of the straightforwardness with which men might deal with their Father. Hence the brevity and conciseness of it:

> In praying use not vain repetitions, as the Gentiles do: for they think that they shall be heard for their much speaking. Be not therefore like unto them: for your

Father knoweth what things ye have need of before ye
ask him. After this manner therefore pray ye:

> Our Father, who art in heaven,
> Hallowed be thy name.
> Thy kingdom come.
> Thy will be done, as in heaven, so on earth.
> Give us this day our daily bread.
> And forgive us our debts, as we also have forgiven our
> debtors. And bring us not into temptation, but deliv-
> er us from the evil one.
> —Matthew 6:7–13 (American Revision)

The Lord's Prayer is so familiar to us that few have stopped to
understand it. The general tragedy of misunderstanding which
has followed Jesus throughout the centuries has frustrated the
purpose of his model prayer also. He gave it to stop vain repe-
titions, and it has been turned into a contrivance for incessant
repetition.

The churches have employed it for their ecclesiastical ritual.
Yet it is not ecclesiastical. There is no hint in it of the Church, the
ministry, the trines of theology, or the sacraments—though the
Latin Vulgate has turned the petition for the daily bread into a
prayer for the "super-substantial bread" of the sacrament.

It has also been used for the devotions of the personal religious life. It is, indeed, profoundly personal. But its deepest significance for the individual is revealed only when he dedicates
his personality to the vaster purposes of the kingdom of God,
and approaches all his personal problems from that point of
view. Then he enters both into the real meaning of the Lord's
Prayer, and into the spirit of the Lord himself.

The Lord's Prayer is part of the heritage of social Christianity
which has been appropriated by men who have had little sympathy with its social spirit. It belongs to the equipment of the
soldiers of the kingdom of God. I wish to claim it here as the
great charter of all social prayers.

When he bade us say, "Our Father," Jesus spoke from that consciousness of human solidarity which was a matter of course in all his thinking. He compels us to clasp hands in spirit with all our brothers and thus to approach the Father together. This rules out all selfish isolation in religion. Before God no man stands alone. Before the All-seeing he is surrounded by the spiritual throng of all to whom he stands related near and far, all whom he loves or hates, whom he serves or oppresses, whom he wrongs or saves. We are one with our fellow-men in all our needs. We are one in our sin and our salvation. To recognize that oneness is the first step toward praying the Lord's Prayer aright. That recognition is also the foundation of social Christianity.

The three petitions with which the prayer begins express the great desire which was fundamental in the heart and mind of Jesus: "Hallowed be thy name. Thy kingdom come. Thy will be done, as in heaven, so on earth." Together they express his yearning faith in the possibility of a reign of God on earth in which his name shall be hallowed and his will be done. They look forward to the ultimate perfection of the common life of humanity on this earth, and pray for the divine revolution which is to bring that about.

There is no request here that we be saved from earthliness and go to heaven which has been the great object of churchly religion. We pray here that heaven may be duplicated on earth through the moral and spiritual transformation of humanity, both in its personal units and its corporate life. No form of religion has ever interpreted this prayer aright which did not have a loving understanding for the plain daily relations of men, and a living faith in their possible spiritual nobility.

And no man has outgrown the crude selfishness of religious immaturity who has not followed Jesus in setting this desire for the social salvation of mankind ahead of all personal desires. The desire for the Kingdom of God precedes and outranks everything else in religion, and forms the tacit presupposition of all our wishes for ourselves. In fact, no one has a clear right to ask for bread for his body or strength for his soul, unless he has identified his will with this all-embracing purpose of God, and intends to use the vitality of body and soul in the attainment of that end.

With that understanding we can say that the remaining petitions deal with personal needs.

Among these the prayer for the daily bread takes first place. Jesus was never as "spiritual" as some of his later followers. He never forgot or belittled the elemental need of men for bread. The fundamental place which he gives to this petition is a recognition of the economic basis of life.

But he lets us pray only for the bread that is needful, and for that only when it becomes needful. The conception of what is needful will expand as human life develops. But this prayer can never be used to cover luxuries that debilitate, nor accumulations of property that can never be used but are sure to curse the soul of the holder with the diverse diseases of mammonism.

In this petition, too, Jesus compels us to stand together. We have to ask in common for our daily bread. We sit at the common table in God's great house, and the supply of each depends on the security of all. The more society is socialized, the clearer does that fact become, and the more just and humane its organization becomes, the more will that recognition be at the bottom of all our institutions. As we stand thus in common, looking up to God for our bread, every one of us ought to feel the sin and shame of it if he habitually takes more than his fair share and leaves others hungry that he may surfeit. It is inhuman, irreligious, and indecent.

The remaining petitions deal with the spiritual needs. Looking backward, we see that our lives have been full of sin and failure, and we realize the need of forgiveness. Looking forward, we tremble at the temptations that await us and pray for deliverance from evil.

In these prayers for the inner life, where the soul seems to confront God alone, we should expect to find only individualistic religion. But even here the social note sounds clearly.

This prayer will not permit us to ask for God's forgiveness without making us affirm that we have forgiven our brothers and are on a basis of brotherly love with all men: "Forgive us our debts, as we also have forgiven our debtors." We shall have to be socially right if we want to be religiously right. Jesus will not suffer us to be pious toward God and merciless toward men.

In the prayer, "Lead us not into temptation," we feel the human trembling of fear. Experience has taught us our frailty. Every man can see certain contingencies just a step ahead of him and knows that his moral capacity for resistance would collapse hopelessly if he were placed in these situations. Therefore, Jesus gives voice to our inarticulate plea to God not to bring us into such situations.

But such situations are created largely by the social life about us. If the society in which we move is rank with sexual looseness, or full of the suggestiveness and solicitations of alcoholism; if our business life is such that we have to lie and cheat and be cruel in order to live and prosper; if our political organization offers an ambitious man the alternative of betraying the public good or of being thwarted and crippled in all his efforts, then the temptations are created in which men go under, and society frustrates the prayer we utter to God. No church can interpret this petition intelligently which closes its mind to the debasing or invigorating influence of the spiritual environment furnished by society. No man can utter this petition without conscious or unconscious hypocrisy who is helping to create the temptations in which others are sure to fall.

The words "Deliver us from the evil one" have in them the ring of battle. They bring to mind the incessant grapple between God and the permanent and malignant powers of evil in humanity. To the men of the first century that meant Satan and his host of evil spirits who ruled in the oppressive, extortionate, and idolatrous powers of Rome. Today the original spirit of that prayer will probably be best understood by those who are pitted against the terrible powers of organized covetousness and institutionalized oppression.

Thus the Lord's Prayer is the great prayer of social Christianity. It is charged with what we call "social consciousness." It assumes the social solidarity of men as a matter of course. It recognizes the social basis of all moral and religious life even in the most intimate personal relations to God. It is not the property of those whose chief religious aim is to pass through an evil world in safety, leaving the world's evil unshaken. Its dominating thought is the moral and religious transformation of mankind in all its social relations. It was left us by Jesus, the great initiator of the Christian revolution; and it is the rightful property of those who follow his banner in the conquest of the world.

INDIVIDUAL PRAYERS

For Children Who Work

O Thou great Father of the weak, lay thy hand tenderly on all the little children on earth and bless them. Bless our own children, who are life of our life, and who have become the heart of our heart. Bless every little childfriend that has leaned against our knee and refreshed our soul by its smiling trustfulness. Be good to all children who long in vain for human love, or for flowers and water, and the sweet breast of Nature. But bless with a sevenfold blessing the young lives whose slender shoulders are already bowed beneath the yoke of toil, and whose glad growth is being stunted forever. Suffer not their little bodies to be utterly sapped, and their minds to be given over to stupidity and the vices of an empty soul. We have all jointly deserved the millstone of thy wrath for making these little ones to stumble and fall. Grant all employers of labor stout hearts to refuse enrichment at such a price. Grant to all the citizens and officers of states which now permit this wrong the grace of holy anger. Help us to realize that every child of our nation is in very truth our child, a member of our great family. By the Holy Child that nestled in Mary's bosom; by the memories of our own childhood joys and sorrows; by the sacred possibilities that slumber in every child, we beseech thee to save us from killing the sweetness of young life by the greed of gain.

For the Children of the Street

O Heavenly Father, whose unveiled face the angels of little children do always behold, look with love and pity, we beseech thee, upon the children of the streets. Where men, in their busy and careless lives, have made a highway, these children of thine have made a home and a school, and are learning the bad lessons of our selfishness and our folly. Save them, and save us, O Lord. Save them from ignorance and brutality, from the shamelessness of lust, the hardness of greed, and the besotting of drink; and save us from the greater guilt of those that offend thy little ones, and from hypocrisy of those that say they see and see not, whose sin remaineth.

Make clear to those of older years the inalienable right of childhood to play, and give to those who govern our cities the will and ability to provide the places for play; make clear to those who minister to the appetite for recreation the guilt of them that lead astray thy children; and make clear to us all that the great school of life is not encompassed by walls and that its teachers are all who influence their younger brethren by companionship and example, whether for good or evil, and that in that school all we are teachers and as we teach are judged. For all false teaching, for all hindering of thy children, pardon us, O Lord, and suffer the little children to come unto thee, for Jesus' sake.

For Women Who Toil

O God, we pray thee for our sisters who are leaving the ancient shelter of the home to earn their wage in the factory and the

---

store amid the press of modern life. Save them from the strain of unremitting toil that would unfit them for the holy duties of home and motherhood which the future may lay upon them. Give them grace to cherish under the new surroundings the old sweetness and gentleness of womanhood, and in the rough mingling of life to keep their hearts pure and their lives untarnished. Save them from the terrors of utter want. Teach them to stand loyally by their sisters, that by united action they may better their common lot.

If it must be so that our women toil like men, help us still to reverence in them the mothers of the future. But make us determined to shield them from unequal burdens, that the women of our nation be not drained of strength and hope for the enrichment of a few, lest our homes grow poor in the wifely sweetness and motherly love which have been the saving strength and glory of our country. To such as yearn for the love and sovereign freedom of their own home, grant in due time the fulfilment of their sweet desires. By Mary, the beloved, who bore the world's redemption in her bosom; by the memory of our own dear mothers who kissed our souls awake; by the little daughters who must soon go out into that world which we are now fashioning for others, we beseech thee that we may deal aright by all women.

For Workingmen

O God, thou mightiest worker of the universe, source of all strength and author of all unity, we pray thee for our brothers, the industrial workers of the nation. As their work binds them together in common toil and danger, may their hearts be knit together in a strong sense of their common interests and destiny. Help them to realize that the injury of one is the concern of all, and that the welfare of all must be the aim of every one. If any of them is tempted to sell the birthright of his class for a mess of pottage for himself, give him a wider outlook and a nobler sympathy with his fellows. Teach them to keep step in a steady onward march, and in their own way to fulfil the law of Christ by bearing the common burdens.

Grant the organizations of labor quiet patience and prudence in all disputes, and fairness to see the other side. Save them from malice and bitterness. Save them from the headlong folly which ruins a fair cause, and give them wisdom resolutely to put aside the two-edged sword of violence that turns on those who seize it. Raise up for them still more leaders of able mind and large heart, and give them grace to follow the wiser counsel.

When they strive for leisure and health and a better wage, do thou grant their cause success, but teach them not to waste their gain on fleeting passions, but to use it in building fairer homes and a nobler manhood. Grant all classes of our nation a larger comprehension for the aspirations of labor and for the courage and worth of these our brothers, that we may cheer them in their struggles and understand them even in their sins. And may the upward climb of Labor, its defeats and its victories, in the farther reaches bless all classes of our nation, and build up for the republic of the future a great body of workers, strong of limb, clear of mind, fair in temper, glad to labor, conscious of their worth, and striving together for the final brotherhood of all men.

For Immigrants

O Thou great Champion of the outcast and the weak, we remember before thee the people of other nations who are coming to our land, seeking bread, a home, and a future. May we look with thy compassion upon those who have been drained and stunted by the poverty and oppression of centuries, and whose minds have been warped by superstition or seared by the dumb agony of revolt. We bless thee for all that America has meant to the alien folk that have crossed the sea in the past, and for all the patient strength and God-fearing courage with which they have enriched our nation. We rejoice in the millions whose life has expanded in the wealth and liberty of our country, and whose children have grown to fairer stature and larger thoughts; for we, too, are the children of immigrants, who came with anxious hearts and halting feet on the westward path of hope.

We beseech thee that our republic may no longer fail their trust. We mourn for the dark sins of past and present, wherein men who are held in honor among us made spoil of the ignorance and helplessness of the strangers and sent them to an early death. In a nation dedicated to liberty may they not find the old oppression and a fiercer greed. May they never find that the arm of the law is but the arm of the strong. Help our whole people henceforth to keep in leash the cunning that would devour the simple. May they feel here the pure air of freedom and face the morning radiance of a joyous hope.

For all the oppressed afar off who sigh for liberty; for all lovers of the people who strive to break their shackles; for all who dare to believe in democracy and the Kingdom of God, make thou our great commonwealth once more a sure beacon-light of hope and a guide on the path which leads to the perfect union of law and liberty.

For Employers

We invoke thy grace and wisdom, O Lord, upon all men of good will who employ and control the labor of men. Amid the numberless irritations and anxieties of their position, help them to keep a quiet and patient temper, and to rule firmly and wisely, without harshness and anger. Since they hold power over the bread, the safety, and the hopes of the workers, may they wield their powers justly and with love, as older brothers and leaders in the great fellowship of labor. Suffer not the heavenly light of compassion for the weak and the old to be quenched in their hearts. When they are tempted to follow the ruthless ways of others, and to sacrifice human health and life for profit, do thou strengthen their will in the hour of need, and bring to naught the

counsels of the heartless. Save them from repressing their workers into sullen submission and helpless fear. May they not sin
against the Christ by using the bodies and souls of men as mere
tools to make things, forgetting the human hearts and longings
of these their brothers.

Raise up among us employers who shall be makers of men as
well as of goods. Give us masters of industry who will use their
higher ability and knowledge in lifting the workers to increasing
independence and vigor, and who will train their helpers for the
larger responsibilities of the coming age. Give us men of faith
who will see beyond the strife of the present and catch a vision
of a nobler organization of our work, when all will still follow
the leadership of the ablest, not in fear but by the glad will of all,
and when none shall be master and none shall be man, but all
shall stand side by side in a strong and righteous brotherhood
of work.

For Men in Business

We plead with thee, O God, for our brothers who are pressed
by the cares and beset by the temptations of business life. We
acknowledge before thee our common guilt for the hardness and
deceitfulness of industry and trade which lead us all into temptation and cause even the righteous to slip and fall. As long as man
is set against man in a struggle for wealth, help the men in business to make their contest, as far as may be, a test of excellence,
by which even the defeated may be spurred to better work. If
any man is pitted against those who have forgotten fairness and
honesty, help him to put his trust resolutely in the profitableness
of sincerity and uprightness, and, if need be, to accept loss rather
than follow on crooked paths.

Establish in unshaken fidelity all who hold in trust the savings of others. Since the wealth and welfare of our nation are
controlled by our business men, cause them to realize that they
serve not themselves alone, but hold high public functions, and

do thou save them from betraying the interests of the many for their own enrichment, lest a new tyranny grow up in a land that is dedicated to freedom. Grant them farsighted patriotism to subordinate their profits to the public weal, and a steadfast determination to transform the disorder of the present into the nobler and freer harmony of the future. May thy Spirit, O God, which is ceaselessly pleading within us, prevail at last to bring our business life under Christ's law of service, so that all who share in the processes of factory and trade may grow up into that high consciousness of a divine calling which blesses those who are the free servants of God and the people and who consciously devote their strength to the common good.

For the Idle

O God, we remember with pain and pity the thousands of our brothers and sisters who seek honest work and seek in vain. For though the unsatisfied wants of men are many, and though our land is wide and calls for labor, yet these thy sons and daughters have no place to labor, and are turned away in humiliation and despair when they seek it. O righteous God, we acknowledge our common guilt for the disorder of our industry which thrusts even willing workers into the degradation of idleness and want, and teaches some to love the sloth which once they feared and hated.

We remember also with sorrow and compassion the idle rich, who have vigor of body and mind and yet produce no useful thing. Forgive them for loading the burden of their support on the bent shoulders of the working world. Forgive them for wasting in refined excess what would feed the pale children of the poor. Forgive them for setting their poisoned splendor before the thirsty hearts of the young, luring them to theft or shame by the lust of eye and flesh. Forgive them for taking pride in their workless lives and despising those by whose toil they live. Forgive them for appeasing their better self by pretended duties and injurious charities. We beseech thee to awaken them by the new voice of thy Spirit that they may look up into the stem eyes of thy Christ and may be smitten with the blessed pangs of repentance. Grant them strength of soul to rise from their silken shame and to give their brothers a just return of labor for the bread they eat. And to our whole nation do thou grant wisdom to create a world in which none shall be forced to idle in want, and none shall be able to idle in luxury, but in which all shall know the health of wholesome work and the sweetness of well-earned rest.

Against War

O Lord, since first the blood of Abel cried to thee from the ground that drank it, this earth of thine has been defiled with the blood of man shed by his brother's hand, and the centuries sob with the ceaseless horror of war. Ever the pride of kings and the covetousness of the strong has driven peaceful nations to slaughter. Ever the songs of the past and the pomp of armies have been used to inflame the passions of the people. Our spirit cries out to thee in revolt against it, and we know that our righteous anger is answered by thy holy wrath.

Break thou the spell of the enchantments that make the nations drunk with the lust of battle and draw them on as willing tools of death. Grant us a quiet and steadfast mind when our own nation clamors for vengeance or aggression. Strengthen our sense of justice and our regard for the equal worth of other peoples and races. Grant to the rulers of nations faith in the possibility of peace through justice, and grant to the common people a new and stem enthusiasm for the cause of peace. Bless our soldiers and sailors for their swift obedience and their willingness to answer to the call of duty, but inspire them none the less with a hatred of war, and may they never for love of private glory or advancement provoke its coming. May our young men still rejoice to die for their country with the valor of their fathers, but teach our age nobler methods of matching our strength and more effective ways of giving our life for the flag.

O thou strong Father of all nations, draw all thy great family together with an increasing sense of our common blood and destiny, that peace may come on earth at last, and thy sun may shed its light rejoicing on a holy brotherhood of peoples.

Against the Servants of Mammon

We cry to thee for justice, O Lord, for our soul is weary with the iniquity of greed. Behold the servants of Mammon, who defy thee and drain their fellow-men for gain; who grind down the strength of the workers by merciless toil and fling them aside when they are mangled and worn; who rack-rent the poor and make dear the space and air which thou hast made free; who paralyze the hand of justice by corruption and blind the eyes of the people by lies; who nullify by their craft the merciful laws which nobler men have devised for the protection of the weak; who have made us ashamed of our dear country by their defilements and have turned our holy freedom into a hollow name; who have brought upon thy Church the contempt of men and have cloaked their extortion with the Gospel of thy Christ.

For the Kingdom of God

O Christ, thou hast bidden us pray for the coming of thy Father's kingdom, in which his righteous will shall be done on earth. We have treasured thy words, but we have forgotten their meaning, and thy great hope has grown dim in thy Church. We bless thee for the inspired souls of all ages who saw afar the shining city of God, and by faith left the profit of the present to follow their vision. We rejoice that to-day the hope of these lonely hearts is becoming the clear faith of millions. Help us, O Lord, in the courage of faith to seize what has now come so near, that the glad day of God may dawn at last. As we have mastered Nature that we might gain wealth, help us now to master the social relations of mankind that we may gain justice and a world of brothers. For what shall it profit our nation if it gain numbers and riches, and lose the sense of the living God and the joy of human brotherhood? Make us determined to live by truth and not by lies, to found our common life on the eternal foundations of righteousness and love, and no longer to prop the tottering house of wrong by legalized cruelty and force. Help us to make the welfare of all the supreme law of our land, that so our commonwealth may be built strong and secure on the love of all its citizens. Cast down the throne of Mammon who ever grinds the life of men, and set up thy throne, O Christ, for thou didst die that men might live. Show thy erring children at last the way from the City of Destruction to the City of Love, and fulfil the longings of the prophets of humanity. Our Master, once more we make thy faith our prayer: "Thy kingdom come! Thy will be done on earth!"

For Those Who Come after Us

O God, we pray thee for those who come after us, for our children, and the children of our friends, and for all the young lives that are marching up from the gates of birth, pure and eager, with the morning sunshine on their faces. We remember with a pang that these will live in the world we are making for them. We are wasting the resources of the earth in our headlong greed, and they will suffer want. We are building sunless houses and joyless cities for our profit, and they must dwell therein. We are making the burden heavy and the pace of work pitiless, and they will fall wan and sobbing by the wayside. We are poisoning the air of our land by our lies and our uncleanness, and they will breathe it.

Grant us grace to leave the earth fairer than we found it; to build upon it cities of God in which the cry of needless pain shall cease; and to put the yoke of Christ upon our business life that it may serve and not destroy. Lift the veil of the future and show us the generation to come as it will be if blighted by our guilt, that our lust may be cooled and we may walk in the fear of the Eternal. Grant us a vision of the far-off years as they may be if redeemed by the sons of God, that we may take heart and do battle for thy children and ours.

For the Prophets and Pioneers

We praise thee, Almighty God, for thine elect, the prophets and martyrs of humanity, who gave their thoughts and prayers and agonies for the truth of God and the freedom of the people. We praise thee that amid loneliness and the contempt of men, in poverty and imprisonment, when they were condemned by the laws of the mighty and buffeted on the scaffold, thou didst uphold them by thy spirit in loyalty to thy holy cause.

Our hearts burn within us as we follow the bleeding feet of thy Christ down the centuries, and count the mounts of anguish on which he was crucified anew in his prophets and the true apostles of his spirit. Help us to forgive those who did it, for some truly thought they were serving thee when they suppressed thy light, but oh, save us from the same mistake! Grant us an unerring instinct for what is right and true, and a swift sympathy to divine those who truly love and serve the people. Suffer us not by thoughtless condemnation or selfish opposition to weaken the arm and chill the spirit of those who strive for the redemption of mankind. May we never bring upon us the blood of all the righteous by renewing the spirit of those who persecuted them in the past. Grant us rather that we, too, may be counted in the chosen band of those who have given their life as a ransom for the many. Send us forth with the pathfinders of humanity to lead thy people another day's march toward the land of promise.

And if we, too, must suffer loss, and drink of the bitter pool of misunderstanding and scorn, uphold us by thy spirit in steadfastness and joy because we are found worthy to share in the work and the reward of Jesus and all the saints.

For the Church

O God, we pray for thy Church, which is set to-day amid the perplexities of a changing order, and face to face with a great new task. We remember with love the nurture she gave to our spiritual life in its infancy, the tasks she set for our growing strength, the influence of the devoted hearts she gathers, the steadfast power for good she has exerted. When we compare her with all other human institutions, we rejoice, for there is none like her. But when we judge her by the mind of her Master, we bow in pity and contrition. Oh, baptize her afresh in the life-giving spirit of Jesus! Grant her a new birth, though it be with the travail of repentance and humiliation. Bestow upon her a more imperious responsiveness to duty, a swifter compassion with suffering, and an utter loyalty to the will of God. Put upon her lips the ancient gospel of her Lord. Help her to proclaim boldly the coming of the Kingdom of God and the doom of all that resist it. Fill her with the prophets' scorn of tyranny, and with a Christlike tenderness for the heavy-laden and down-trodden. Give her faith to espouse the cause of the people, and in their hands that grope after freedom and light to recognize the bleeding hands of the Christ. Bid her cease from seeking her own life, lest she lose it. Make her valiant to give up her life to humanity, that like her crucified Lord she may mount by the path of the cross to a higher glory.

For Our City

O God, we pray thee for this, the city of our love and pride. We rejoice in her spacious beauty and her busy ways of commerce, in her stores and factories where hand joins hand in toil, and in her blessed homes where heart joins heart for rest and love.

We thank thee for the patriot men and women of the past whose generous devotion to the common good has been the making of our city. Grant that our own generation may build worthily on the foundation they have laid. If in the past there have been some who have sold the city's good for private gain, staining her honor by their cunning and greed, fill us, we beseech thee, with the righteous anger of true sons that we may purge out the shame lest it taint the future years.

Grant us a vision of our city, fair as she might be: a city of justice, where none shall prey on others; a city of plenty, where vice and poverty shall cease to fester; a city of brotherhood, where all success shall be founded on service, and honor shall be given to nobleness alone; a city of peace, where order shall not rest on force, but on the love of all for the city, the great mother of the common life and weal. Hear thou, O Lord, the silent prayer of all our hearts as we each pledge our time and strength and thought to speed the day of her coming beauty and righteousness.

For the Cooperative Commonwealth

Bring to an end, O Lord, the inhumanity of the present, in which all men are ridden by the pale fear of want while the nation of which they are citizens sits throned amid the wealth of their making; when the manhood in some is cowed by helplessness, while the soul of others is surfeited and sick with power which no frail son of the dust should wield.

O God, save us, for our nation is at strife with its own soul and is sinning against the light which thou aforetime hast kindled in it. Thou hast called our people to freedom, but we are withholding from men their share in the common heritage without which freedom becomes a hollow name. Thy Christ has kindled in us the passion for brotherhood, but the social life we have built, denies and slays brotherhood.

We pray thee to revive in us the hardy spirit of our forefathers that we may establish and complete their work, building on the basis of their democracy the firm edifice of a cooperative commonwealth, in which both government and industry shall be of the people, by the people, and for the people. May we, who now live, see the oncoming of the great day of God, when all men shall stand side by side in equal worth and real freedom, all toiling and all reaping, masters of nature but brothers of men, exultant in the tide of the common life, and jubilant in the adoration of thee, the source of their blessings and the Father of all.

Morituri Te Salutant

O Thou Eternal One, we who are doomed to die lift up our souls to thee for strength, for Death has passed us in the throng of men and touched us, and we know that at some turn of our pathway he stands waiting to take us by the hand and lead us— we know not whither. We praise thee that to us he is no more an enemy but thy great angel and our friend, who alone can open for some of us the prison-house of pain and misery and set our feet in the roomy spaces of a larger life. Yet we are but children, afraid of the dark and the unknown, and we dread the parting from the life that is so sweet and from the loved ones who are so dear.

Grant us of thy mercy a valiant heart, that we may tread the road with head uplifted and a smiling face. May we do our work to the last with a wholesome joy, and love our loves with an added tenderness because the days of love are short. On thee we cast the heaviest burden that numbs our soul, the gnawing fear for those we love, whom we must leave unsheltered in a selfish world. We trust in thee, for through all our years thou hast been our stay. O thou Father of the fatherless, put thy arm about our little ones! And ere we go, we pray that the days may come when the dying may die unafraid, because men have ceased to prey on the weak, and the great family of the nation enfolds all with its strength and care.

We thank thee that we have tasted the rich life of humanity. We bless thee for every hour of life, for all our share in the joys and strivings of our brothers, for the wisdom gained which will be part of us forever. If soon we must go, yet through thee we have lived and our life flows on in the race. By thy grace we too have helped to shape the future and bring in the better day.

If our spirit droops in loneliness, uphold us by thy companionship. When all the voices of love grow faint and drift away, thy everlasting arms will still be there. Thou art the father of our spirits; from thee we have come; to thee we go. We rejoice that in the hours of our purer vision, when the pulse-throb of thine eternity is strong within us, we know that no pang of mortality can reach our unconquerable soul, and that for those who abide in thee death is but the gateway to life eternal. Into thy hands we commend our spirit.

7

The Superpersonal Forces of Evil

This work is from Chapter VIII of Rauschenbusch's A Theology for the Social Gospel *(1917). In this, his last book, he has several chapters on the reality of sin in history. Contrary to his later critics, Rauschenbusch did not believe that sin would eventually be eliminated from human affairs. Far from the liberal idealist that some thought him to be, he knew the depth of evil in human affairs, especially in the domains of economics and politics.*

Individualistic theology has not trained the spiritual intelligence of Christian men and women to recognize and observe spiritual entities beyond the individual. Our religious interest has been so focused on the soul of the individual and its struggles that we have remained uneducated as to the more complex units of spiritual life.

The chief exception to this statement is our religious insight into the history of Israel and Judah, into the nature of the family, and the qualities of the Church. The first of these we owe to the solidaristic vision of the Old Testament prophets who saw their nation as a gigantic personality which sinned, suffered, and repented. The second we owe to the deep interest which the Church from the beginning has taken in the purity of family life and the Christian nurture of the young. The third we owe to the high valuation the Church has always put on itself. It has claimed a continuous and enduring life of its own which enfolds all its members and distinguishes it from every other organization and from the totality of the worldly life outside of it. It is hard to deny this. Not only have the Church as a whole, but distinctive groups and organizations within the Church, such as the Friends or the Jesuit Order, maintained their own character and principles tenaciously against all influences. This is the noblest view that we can take of the Church—that the spirit of her Lord has always been an informing principle of life within her, and that, though faltering, sinning, and defiled, she has kept her own collective personality intact. Paul's discussion of the Church as the body of Christ (1 Cor. 12) is the first and classical discussion in Christian thought of the nature and functioning of a composite spiritual organism.

The Church is not the only organism of that kind, though pre-eminent among them all. Others are less permanent, less distinctive, less attractive, and less self-assertive, but the spiritual self-consciousness of the Church is built up on the social self-consciousness which it shares with other social organisms.

If "the love of money is the root of all evil" and if selfishness is the essence of sin, such an expansion of the range and storage capacity of selfishness must necessarily mark a new era in the history of sin, just as the invention of the steam-engine marked a new era in the production of wealth. Drink, over-eating, sexualism, vanity, and idleness are still reliable standardized sins. But the exponent of gigantic evil on the upper ranges of sin, is the love of money and the love of power over men which property connotes. This is the most difficult field of practical redemption and the most necessitous chance of evangelism.

The theological doctrine of original sin is an important effort to see sin in its totality and to explain its unbroken transmission and perpetuation. But this explanation of the facts is very fragmentary, and theology has done considerable harm in concentrating the attention of religious minds on the biological transmission of evil. It has diverted our minds from the power

of social transmission, from the authority of the social group in
justifying, urging, and idealizing wrong, and from the decisive
influence of economic profit in the defense and propagation of
evil. These are ethical facts, but they have the greatest religious
importance, and they have just as much right to being discussed
in theology as the physical propagation of the species, or cre-
ationism and traducianism. There is the more inducement to
teach clearly on the social transmission and perpetuation of sin
because the ethical and religious forces can really do something
to check and prevent the transmission of sin along social chan-
nels, whereas the biological transmission of original sin, except
for the possible influence of eugenics, seems to be beyond our
influence.

These super-personal forces count in the moral world not
only through their authority over their members, but through
their influence in the general social life. They front the world
outside of them. Their real object usually lies outside. The assim-
ilative power they exert over their members is only their form of
discipline by which they bring their collective body into smooth
and efficient working order. They are the most powerful ethical
forces in our communities.

Evil collective forces have usually fallen from a better estate.
Organizations are rarely formed for avowedly evil ends. They
drift into evil under sinister leadership, or under the pressure of
need or temptation. For instance, a small corrupt group in a city
council, in order to secure control, tempts the weak, conciliates
and serves good men, and turns the council itself into a force of
evil in the city; an inside ring in the police force grafts on the
vice trade, and draws a part of the force into protecting crime
and brow-beating decent citizens; a trade union fights for the
right to organize a shop, but resorts to violence and terroriz-
ing; a trust, desiring to steady prices and to get away from anti-
quated competition, undersells the independents and evades or
purchases legislation. This tendency to deterioration shows the
soundness of the social instincts, but also the ease with which

they go astray, and the need of righteous social institutions to prevent temptation.

In the previous chapter it was pointed out that the love of gain is one of the most unlimited desires and the most inviting outlet for sinful selfishness. The power of combination lends itself to extortion. Predatory profit or graft, when once its sources are opened up and developed, constitutes an almost overwhelming temptation to combinations of men. Its pursuit gives them cohesion and unity of mind, capacity to resist common dangers, and an outfit of moral and political principles which will justify their anti-social activities. The aggressive and defensive doings of such combinations are written all over history. History should be re-written to explain the nature of human parasitism. It would be a revelation. The Roman publican, who collected the taxes from conquered provinces on a contract basis; the upper class in all slave-holding communities; the landlord class in all ages and countries, such as East Prussia, Ireland, Italy, and Russia; the great trading companies in the early history of commerce; these are instances of social groups consolidated by extortionate gain. Such groups necessarily resist efforts to gain political liberty or social justice, for liberty and justice do away with unearned incomes. Their malign influence on the development of humanity has been beyond telling. . . .

The social gospel realizes the importance and power of the super-personal forces in the community. It has succeeded in awakening the social conscience of the nation to the danger of allowing such forces to become parasitic and oppressive. A realization of the spiritual power and value of these composite personalities must get into theology, otherwise theology will not deal adequately with the problem of sin and of redemption, and will be unrelated to some of the most important work of salvation which the coming generations will have to do.

8

The Challenge of the Social Gospel
to Theology

This is chapter 1 of Rauschenbusch's last book, A Theology for
the Social Gospel *(1917).*

We have a social gospel. We need a systematic theology large
enough to match it and vital enough to back it.

This is the main proposition of this book. The first three chapters are to show that a readjustment and expansion of theology, so that it will furnish an adequate intellectual basis for the
social gospel, is necessary, feasible, desirable, and legitimate. The
remainder of the book offers concrete suggestions how some
of the most important sections of doctrinal theology may be
expanded and readjusted to make room for the religious convictions summed up in "the social gospel."

Some of my readers, who know the age, the tenacity, and the
monumental character of theology well, will smile at the audac-
ity of this proposal. Others, who know theology still better, will
treat this venture very seriously. If theology stops growing or is
unable to adjust itself to its modern environment and to meet
its present tasks, it will die. Many now regard it as dead. The
social gospel needs a theology to make it effective; but theology
needs the social gospel to vitalize it. The work attempted in this
book is doomed to futility if it has only the personal ideas of the

author behind it. It is worthy of consideration only if the needs of a new epoch are seeking expression in it, and in that case its personal defects are of slight importance.

The argument of this book is built on the conviction that the social gospel is a permanent addition to our spiritual outlook and that its arrival constitutes a stage in the development of the Christian religion.

We need not waste words to prove that the social gospel is being preached. It is no longer a prophetic and occasional note. It is a novelty only in backward social or religious communities. The social gospel has become orthodox.

It is not only preached. It has set new problems for local church work, and has turned the pastoral and organizing work of the ministry into new and constructive directions. It has imparted a wider vision and a more statesmanlike grasp to the foreign mission enterprise. In home missions its advent was signalized by the publication, in 1885, of "Our Country" by Josiah Strong. (*Venerabile nomen!*) That book lifted the entire home mission problem to a higher level. The religious literature uttering the social gospel is notable both for its volume and its vitality and conviction. The emotional fervor of the new convictions has created prayers and hymns of social aspiration, for which the newer hymn books are making room. Conservative denominations have formally committed themselves to the fundamental ideas of the social gospel and their practical application. The plans of great interdenominational organizations are inspired by it. It has become a constructive force in American politics.

This new orientation, which is observable in all parts of our religious life, is not simply a prudent adjustment of church methods to changed conditions. There is religious compulsion behind it. Those who are in touch with the student population know what the impulse to social service means to college men and women. It is the most religious element in the life of many of them. Among ministerial students there is an almost impatient demand for a proper social outlet. Some hesitate to enter the regular ministry at all because they doubt whether it will offer them sufficient opportunity and freedom to utter and apply their social convictions. For many ministers who have come under the influence of the social gospel in mature years, it has signified a religious crisis, and where it has been met successfully, it has brought fresh joy and power, and a distinct enlargement of mind. It has taken the place of conventional religion in the lives of many outside the Church. It constitutes the moral power in the propaganda of Socialism.

All those social groups which distinctly face toward the future, clearly show their need and craving for a social interpretation and application of Christianity. Whoever wants to hold audiences of working people must establish some connection between religion and their social feelings and experiences. The religious organizations dealing with college men and women know that any appeal which leaves out the social note is likely to meet a listless audience. The most effective evangelists for these two groups are men who have thoroughly embodied the social gospel in their religious life and thought. When the great evangelistic effort of the "Men and Religion Forward Movement" was first planned, its organizers made room for "Social Service" very hesitatingly. But as soon as the movement was tried out before the public, it became clear that only the meetings which offered the people the social application of religion were striking fire and drawing crowds.

The Great War has dwarfed and submerged all other issues, including our social problems. But in fact the war is the most acute and tremendous social problem of all. All whose Christianity has not been ditched by the catastrophe are demanding a christianizing of international relations. The demand for disarmament and permanent peace, for the rights of the small nations against the imperialistic and colonizing powers, for freedom of the seas and of trade routes, for orderly settlement of grievances, these are demands for social righteousness and fraternity on the largest scale. Before the War the social gospel dealt with social classes; to-day it is being translated into international terms. The ultimate cause of the war was the same lust for easy and unearned gain which has created the internal social evils under which every nation has suffered. The social problem and the war problem are fundamentally one problem, and the social gospel faces both. After the War the social gospel will "come back" with pent-up energy and clearer knowledge.

The social movement is the most important ethical and spiritual movement in the modern world, and the social gospel is the response of the Christian consciousness to it. Therefore it had to be. The social gospel registers the fact that for the first time in history the spirit of Christianity has had a chance to form a working partnership with real social and psychological science. It is the religious reaction on the historic advent of democracy. It seeks to put the democratic spirit, which the Church inherited from Jesus and the prophets, once more in control of the institutions and teachings of the Church.

The social gospel is the old message of salvation, but enlarged and intensified. The individualistic gospel has taught us to see the sinfulness of every human heart and has inspired us with faith in the willingness and power of God to save every soul that comes to him. But it has not given us an adequate understanding of the sinfulness of the social order and its share in the sins of all individuals within it. It has not evoked faith in the will and power of God to redeem the permanent institutions of human society from their inherited guilt of oppression and extortion. Both our sense of sin and our faith in salvation have fallen short of the realities under its teaching. The social gospel seeks to bring men under repentance for their collective sins and to create a more sensitive and more modern conscience. It calls on us for the faith of the old prophets who believed in the salvation of nations.

Now, if this insight and religious outlook become common to large and vigorous sections of the Christian Church, the solutions of life contained in the old theological system will seem puny and inadequate. Our faith will be larger than the intellectual system which subtends it. Can theology expand to meet the growth of faith? The biblical studies have responded to the spiritual hunger aroused by the social gospel. The historical interpretation of the Bible has put the religious personalities, their spiritual struggles, their growth, and their utterances, into social connection with the community life of which they were part. This method of interpretation has given back the Bible to men of modernized intelligence and has made it the feeder of faith in the social gospel. The studies of "practical theology" are all in a process of rejuvenation and expansion in order to create competent leadership for the Church, and most of these changes are due to the rise of new ideals created by the social gospel. What, then, will doctrinal theology do to meet the new situation? Can it ground and anchor the social gospel in the eternal truths of our religion and build its main ideas into the systematic structure of Christian doctrine?

Theology is not superior to the gospel. It exists to aid the preaching of salvation. Its business is to make the essential facts and principles of Christianity so simple and dear, so adequate and mighty, that all who preach or teach the gospel, both ministers and laymen, can draw on its stores and deliver a complete and unclouded Christian message. When the progress of humanity creates new tasks, such as world-wide missions, or new problems, such as the social problem, theology must connect these with the old fundamentals of our faith and make them Christian tasks and problems.

The adjustment of the Christian message to the regeneration of the social order is plainly one of the most difficult tasks ever laid on the intellect of religious leaders. The pioneers of the social gospel have had a hard time trying to consolidate their old faith and their new aim. Some have lost their faith; others have come out of the struggle with crippled formulations of truth. Does not our traditional theology deserve some of the blame for this spiritual wastage because it left these men without spiritual support and allowed them to become the vicarious victims of our theological inefficiency?

If our theology is silent on social salvation, we compel college men and women, workingmen, and theological students, to choose between an unsocial system of theology and an irreligious system of social salvation. It is not hard to predict the outcome. If we seek to keep Christian doctrine unchanged, we shall ensure its abandonment.

Instead of being an aid in the development of the social gospel, systematic theology has often been a real clog. When a minister speaks to his people about child labor or the exploitation of the lowly by the strong; when he insists on adequate food, education, recreation, and a really human opportunity for all, there is response. People are moved by plain human feeling and by the instinctive convictions which they have learned from Jesus Christ. But at once there are doubting and dissenting voices. We are told that environment has no saving power; regeneration is what men need; we cannot have a regenerate society without regenerate individuals; we do not live for this world but for the life to come; it is not the function of the church to deal with economic questions; any effort to change the social order before the coming of the Lord is foredoomed to failure. These objections all issue from the theological consciousness created by traditional church teaching. These half-truths are the proper product of a half-way system of theology in which there is no room for social redemption. Thus the Church is halting between two voices that call it. On the one side is the voice of the living Christ amid living men to-day; on the other side is the voice of past ages embodied in theology. Who will say that the authority of this voice has never confused our Christian judgment and paralyzed our determination to establish God's kingdom on earth?

Those who have gone through the struggle for a clear faith in the social gospel would probably agree that the doctrinal theology in which they were brought up, was one of the most baffling hindrances in their spiritual crisis, and that all their mental energies were taxed to overcome the weight of its traditions. They were fortunate if they promptly discovered some recent theological book which showed them at least the possibility of conceiving Christian doctrine in social terms, and made them conscious of a fellowship of faith in their climb toward the light. The situation would be much worse if Christian thought were nourished on doctrine only. Fortunately our hymns and prayers have a richer consciousness of solidarity than individualistic theology. But even to-day many ministers have a kind of dumb-bell system of thought, with the social gospel at one end and individual salvation at the other end, and an attenuated connection between them. The strength of our faith is in its unity. Religion wants wholeness of life. We need a rounded system of doctrine large enough to take in all our spiritual interests.

In short, we need a theology large enough to contain the social gospel, and alive and productive enough not to hamper it.

MODERN SPIRITUAL MASTERS
Robert Ellsberg, Series Editor

This series introduces the essential writing and vision of some of the great spiritual teachers of our time. While many of these figures are rooted in long-established traditions of spirituality, others have charted new, untested paths. In each case, however, they have engaged in a spiritual journey shaped by the challenges and concerns of our age. Together with the saints and witnesses of previous centuries, these modern spiritual masters may serve as guides and companions to a new generation of seekers.

Already published:

Modern Spiritual Masters (edited by Robert Ellsberg)
Swami Abhishiktananda (edited by Shirley du Boulay)
Metropolitan Anthony of Sourozh (edited by Gillian Crow)
Eberhard Arnold (edited by Johann Christoph Arnold)
Pedro Arrupe (edited by Kevin F. Burke, S.J.)
Daniel Berrigan (edited by John Dear)
Thomas Berry (edited by Mary EvelynTucker and John Grim)
Dietrich Bonhoeffer (edited by Robert Coles)
Robert McAfee Brown (edited by Paul Crowley)
Dom Helder Camara (edited by Francis McDonagh)
Carlo Carretto (edited by Robert Ellsberg)
G. K. Chesterton (edited by William Griffin)
Joan Chittister (edited by Mary Lou Kownacki and Mary Hembrow Snyder)
Yves Congar (edited by Paul Lakeland)
The Dalai Lama (edited by Thomas A. Forsthoefel)
Alfred Delp, S.J. (introduction by Thomas Merton)
Catherine de Hueck Dogerty (edited by David Meconi, S.J.)
Virgilio Elizondo (edited by Timothy Matovina)
Jacques Ellul (edited by Jacob E. Van Vleet)
Ralph Waldo Emerson (edited by Jon M. Sweeney)
Charles de Foucauld (edited by Robert Ellsberg)
Mohandas Gandhi (edited by John Dear)
Bede Griffiths (edited by Thomas Matus)
Romano Guardini (edited by Robert A. Krieg)
Gustavo Gutiérrez (edited by Daniel G. Groody)
Thich Nhat Hanh (edited by Robert Ellsberg)
Abraham Joshua Heschel (edited by Susannah Heschel)
Etty Hillesum (edited by Annemarie S. Kidder)

Caryll Houselander (edited by Wendy M. Wright)
Pope John XXIII (edited by Jean Maalouf)
Rufus Jones (edited by Kerry Walters)
Clarence Jordan (edited by Joyce Hollyday)
Walter Kasper (edited by Patricia C. Bellm and Robert A. Krieg)
John Main (edited by Laurence Freeman)
James Martin (edited by James T. Keane)
Anthony de Mello (edited by William Dych, S.J.)
Thomas Merton (edited by Christine M. Bochen)
John Muir (edited by Tim Flinders)
John Henry Newman (edited by John T. Ford, C.S.C.)
Henri Nouwen (edited by Robert A. Jonas)
Flannery O'Connor (edited by Robert Ellsberg)
Karl Rahner (edited by Philip Endean)
Walter Rauschenbusch (edited by Joseph J. Fahey)
Brother Roger of Taizé (edited by Marcello Fidanzio)
Richard Rohr (edited by Joelle Chase and Judy Traeger)
Oscar Romero (by Marie Dennis, Rennie Golden, and Scott Wright)
Joyce Rupp (edited by Michael Leach)
Albert Schweitzer (edited by James Brabazon)
Frank Sheed and Maisie Ward (edited by David Meconi)
Jon Sobrino (edited by Robert Lassalle-Klein)
Sadhu Sundar Singh (edited by Charles E. Moore)
Mother Maria Skobtsova (introduction by Jim Forest)
Dorothee Soelle (edited by Dianne L. Oliver)
Jon Sobrino (edited by Robert Lasalle-Klein)
Edith Stein (edited by John Sullivan, O.C.D.)
David Steindl-Rast (edited by Clare Hallward)
William Stringfellow (edited by Bill Wylie-Kellerman)
Pierre Teilhard de Chardin (edited by Ursula King)
Mother Teresa (edited by Jean Maalouf)
St. Thérèse of Lisieux (edited by Mary Frohlich)
Phyllis Tickle (edited by Jon M. Sweeney)
Henry David Thoreau (edited by Tim Flinders)
Howard Thurman (edited by Luther E. Smith)
Leo Tolstoy (edited by Charles E. Moore)
Evelyn Underhill (edited by Emilie Griffin)
Vincent Van Gogh (by Carol Berry)
Jean Vanier (edited by Carolyn Whitney-Brown)
Swami Vivekananda (edited by Victor M. Parachin)
Simone Weil (edited by Eric O. Springsted)
John Howard Yoder (edited by Paul Martens and Jenny Howells)